WINSTON, CHURCHILL & ME

a memoir of childhood
1944-1950

BY

JONATHAN DUDLEY

for Eva,
Dóra and Réka

Published by Skyscraper Publications Limited
20 Crab Tree Close, Bloxham, OX15 4SE
www.skyscraperpublications.com

First published 2017

A CIP catalogue record for this book is available
from the British Library.

ISBN-13: 978-1-9110721-9-5

Cover design and typesetting by
Chandler Book Design

Printed in the United Kingdom
by CPI

CONTENTS

INTRODUCTION

This story is driven by the curious invitation I received from the schoolboy whose desk I shared at the pre-prep school we both attended in London. The boy's name was Winston Churchill, that was all I knew at the time. One day in the Spring term of 1949 - when he and I were eight years old - he told me that his grandmother wanted him to bring a "little friend" with him when he went to stay at their house in Kent during the summer. He wanted to know whether I would like to be that friend.

I said I would. It turned out that his grandfather was the famous Winston Churchill.

Even before I met Mr Churchill I thought of him as "Mr Churchill" - not so surprising since this was the extent of his title before he received his knighthood from the Queen in 1953. When I first met him in 1949, nearly four years after the end of the Second World War, I always called him "Sir" to his face, but I continued to think of him and refer to him as "Mr Churchill". Old habits are mighty difficult to break. So throughout this story I refer to the Great Man, Sir Winston or, to give him his full title Sir Winston Leonard Spencer-Churchill KG, OM, CH, TD, PC, DL, FRS, RA, as "Mr Churchill".

In the same way, I still think of Dame Clementine Churchill GBE as "Mrs Churchill", for that is how I referred to her both in 1949 and 1950. Actually she had become Dame Clementine in 1946, but continued to style herself "Mrs Winston Churchill" from 1946 until 1953 when Mr Churchill became Sir Winston Churchill. It was then that she used the title Lady Churchill.

To avoid any possible confusion, I always refer to my classmate Winston Churchill as "Winston".

1

WAR

I don't suppose there was a single moment when Mr. Churchill made the decision to take my hand. Perhaps I was pushing too far ahead of him in my desire to get to the front of the balcony railings so I could get the best view of what was going on below. There were hundreds and hundreds of people crowding outside the house in Hyde Park Gate and we could see them all from our vantage point on the first floor balcony. Everyone was cheering Mr. Churchill, calling his name and waving Conservative Party banners - for this was August 1949 and there was to be a general election, the second since the end of the war, in the following February. I was eight at the time, and so caught up in the spirit of this election rally that I heard myself almost shout out to Mr. Churchill as he waved and smiled and gave his famous V-sign "Golly! This is - Oh Gosh!" He didn't say anything for a while, just continued holding my hand and waving his cigar to the crowd. Then, suddenly, from nowhere he turned his head very slightly towards me and said, "We're not going to win this one."

This was the very last day of my first short holiday staying with the Churchill family. My classmate Winston had asked me if I'd like to go and stay with him at Chartwell, his grandparents' home in Kent, when he went down there in August and I had enjoyed myself very much. When our holiday was over and it was time for me to return home, Mrs. Churchill told us boys that she and Mr. Churchill were going to drive us to London in the car. They had a house in Hyde Park Gate, and it had been arranged that my mother would come round and collect me at tea time. We wouldn't have to set off too early, but Mr. Churchill had agreed to wave to some Conservative Party supporters and say a few words to them at about 2.00pm. Mrs. Churchill said we were to get ready to leave Chartwell soon after breakfast. And that is what we did.

When Mr. Churchill said "We're not going to win this one" I was astonished. I wanted to say "Not going to win? Look how many people are shouting and cheering you on to victory. How could you possibly NOT win?" But I said nothing. It seemed important to think, to make sense of what Mr. Churchill had just told me. Suddenly I felt stupid. "How can you possibly know who's going to win?" I wanted to ask him - for I had it in my mind that on election day everyone goes to vote on the same day and you don't actually know who's won until all the votes are counted. I might ask Winston when we got together later. But it didn't seem to be the kind of thing Winston would know much about.

I thought I'd probably wait until I saw my grandfather and ask him about it. It was certainly difficult for me to believe, on the evidence of the mass of excited people squashed into Hyde Park Gate on that bright afternoon in August 1949, that Mr. Churchill and the Conservative Party were not going to win the general election in

February. And then another thing popped into my mind: my grandfather had told me that when the Second World War was going on and there had been a period when the war hadn't been going at all well for the Allies - a "set-back", I think he called it - lots of people in Britain didn't think Mr. Churchill could possibly pull the country round and win. But he did. He was "a great war leader" my grandfather had said. "Without him, we might very well have lost the war."

I don't remember very much about the war. Things I do remember tend to have happened - unless I have merely imagined them - either at or near the end of the war. My brother Robert was born in March 1944 and soon afterwards my father must have come home on leave because my first memory is set in a nondescript house in Northwood, just outside London. This was the house where my father was billeted when he came back for a short period of leave and my mother, Nanny, Robert and I were there too when, on this particular night, Nanny woke me up and we looked out of the bedroom window at what looked like a giant lozenge floating in the night sky. There were searchlights crisscrossing each other as they tracked the progress of a V1 buzz bomb towards London and the heavy thudding of anti-aircraft guns. I could sense that Nanny's usual composure was disturbed by the flying bomb: she hurried me downstairs, past the pram in the entrance hall to the front room where my mother and father were talking.

Nanny was the centre of my world, just as she would be for the next six or seven years. Her real name was Mary Purdie. She had a younger sister Annie who continued to live and work in the Lake District after Mary had said good-bye to her family in Bowness and travelled south to Liverpool to take up her first paid job as Nanny.

This would be somewhere around 1924, when Nanny, and this has to be an approximation, was in her early twenties. It's an approximation because, whenever Robert and I asked her, as we often did, how old she was at that time - or indeed how old she was right now - she would only ever reply "as old as my tongue and a little older than my teeth". She had been employed in Liverpool by Bertie and Olga Stern to look after their two young daughters. Bertie and Olga were to become my grandparents: Barbara, the elder of their two daughters, was my Mum. I often wondered what Nanny looked like then when she was a young woman caring for my mother in the 1920s. It's odd that throughout the time that Robert and I knew and loved her her appearance seemed not to change at all. Indeed, from my very first remembrance of her in the middle of that night in Northwood when I was three to visiting her in a Windermere nursing home when I was thirty-three she still looked very much the same.

Nanny

Michael and Barbara

My mother Barbara, whose own mother Olga believed that a caring Nanny and elite finishing schools in Switzerland were all a girl really needed to make a good marriage, grew up to be an admired and attractive young woman. Bitter bouts of temper and an enduring frustration with Olga characterised her dark side: she had wanted so much more attention, love and approval from her fashionable, socialite mother than she was ever going to get. War was declared when Barbara, who had done the finishing schools, done the Debutante Season in London, done all the parties with eligible young men, was twenty. In the same year she married Michael Dudley, who, having done all the same parties with eligible young women, was now a commissioned officer in the Irish Guards. He was twenty-three.

When I was born in January 1941 Barbara had no hesitation in inviting Nanny to come back and rejoin the family: Nanny would look after me. By this time, if my approximate date line is to be believed, Nanny would be in her early forties.

Michael, my father, had joined up to fight in the war from its outset. As a young man he was a resolute opponent of fascism: he created a stir when, in his final year at Oxford, he made a rousing speech at a Union Debate urging his contemporaries to take up arms against Hitler. When he married Barbara, he arranged for her to spend the period of the war staying with his parents in their big manor house in Hampshire. Then, when I was born, these grandparents of mine, absolutely devoted to Michael their only son, were only too happy to have me and Nanny to stay as well.

I have quite vivid memories of the impact of the war upon the tiny village of Linkenholt in Hampshire, where I spent most of the time between 1941 and 1945. My father had come home for a short spell of leave one summer and I remember sitting with him and my mother on a rug by the fish pond. We watched the huge number of frogs and tadpoles swimming about and I have a feeling it must have been the day my father was going back to the war because he was wearing a khaki suit. I know this because I remember lying back in his arms, fascinated by the smell of his uniform and playing with the shiny leather of his Sam Browne belt. Later, at the beginning of

1945, when it became clear that the Allies were winning the war in Europe and that peace would soon be declared, my grandparents had a flagpole put up at the mid-point of their long front lawn to greet my father's return.

Linkenholt

Once, probably well before the flagpole was put up, there were strong winds and gales in that part of the Home Counties. Airmen in a US bomber had been practising parachute jumps on some kind of training exercise, the aircraft had been blown off course in the gales and the men had come hurtling out of the sky onto different parts of my grandparents' garden. When Nanny and I were allowed into the hall to see those who had been patched up and brought up to the Manor for a cup of tea, many of the wounded wore huge white bandages on broken legs or arms. Some had landed in trees, others on the heated greenhouses, crashed through the glass roofs and sustained cuts and lacerations. I could see blotches of blood seeping through the white bandages. It was a transfixing experience: there was no chance I could say Hello, no chance I could say anything. These young men were, without exception, extremely polite and clearly grateful for whatever hospitality my grandparents were providing, yet the situation came across to me as ugly and foreign and, in some way, strangely menacing.

The flagpole didn't stay up for very long. I remember the morning in early May 1945 and the motorcyclist arriving. I saw him hand over a small yellowish envelope, and Nanny taking me away out of there, out of the house into the garden where she tried to distract me from the screams of devastating loss and the sight of my mother's face wet and swollen with grief. I knew that something terrible must have happened and I guessed it had to be about my father, But I didn't know then, of course, that on 9th April Michael Dudley had been killed by a sniper's bullet. He was shot in his tank leading the Irish Guards battalion in an assault on German positions at a little place called Fürstenau - for a very short time Fürstenau found itself blocking the 32nd Guards Division's implacable advance towards Berlin. Nor did I get anywhere near to comprehending the bitter timing of his death: VE day was celebrated just twenty-nine days later on May 8th. When my father was killed he was twenty-eight, my mother was twenty-five, I was four and my brother Robert was one.

Immediately after the war my mother took Nanny, my brother and me away from Linkenholt to London. We lived in a house her parents had bought for her in Flood Street, Chelsea. Each day I used to walk with Nanny and the pram to a school called Mitford Colmer - a girls' day school in Eaton Gate which took posh little boys for a brief period - a year or maybe two - before they went on to their pre-prep schools. I was five when I went there. There were two Miss Colmers and one of them, maybe the older sister, would blithely present herself with a drip hanging from the end of her nose. In the mornings a number of much older girls would come and join the little ones and the juniors in the large front room which doubled as an assembly hall. There would be one or two prayers and we would sing There is a Green Hill Far Away or some other popular hymn and then the big girls would leave and we five year olds would have a lesson with dancing the hornpipe in it. PE was usually bending over in a line with other bent-over boys and girls so that we could pass a large ball, volley-ball size, between our legs backwards. Once I was sitting on the lavatory when the door was flung open, I was yanked off the seat by a large woman and thrown out of the door because some little girl needed to be sick. There was a large shiny map of the world pinned up on our classroom wall. Nothing else from the school has stuck in my memory - except the long, grey walk with Nanny and Robert's pram back to Flood Street.

London at that time was tinted grey, street by street, everywhere you looked. The colour brightened a little in sunshine, but was always and everywhere grey. In the winter months, when fires were lit and thick grey smoke drifted out of a great many household chimneys, the afternoons turned out foggy, and quite often our walk home after school was through this hazardous, dirty-tasting atmosphere. On some days the fog was so thick we couldn't see more than five or six yards ahead of us. Churches rang their bells almost continually, funerals or memorial services perhaps. Bomb damage was widespread, the dereliction often stark, the buildings crushed and gaping. Once my mother took me with her to see a bank manager in Cavendish Square. We went on a bus which had to navigate safe passage between and around the bomb craters along Oxford Street. When we arrived at the bank, the manager took us into his office at the back of the building. I didn't listen to their conversation as he talked with my mother about money things but he captured my attention when I heard him call my mother a "naughty girl": "You've been a very naughty girl," he said. I think he said it more than once or twice and I began to cry. There was something disturbing not so much about what he said but about the way he said it. As if this was an episode of highly charged if not aggressive flirting with my mother which, in my young view, was totally out of order. Maybe I believed he was posing a threat to the delicate and newfound stability of our lives. I don't know - but my crying was enough to prompt my mother to say goodbye to this horrible man, to get hold of my hand and take me home on the bus and back to Nanny.

In the time between coming to London in late 1945 and going to my pre-prep school Gibbs in the autumn of 1946 I kept secret watch for my father's return. While all the grown-ups, including Nanny, seemed to accept the bad news that he was dead, I wasn't so sure about that. In my bedroom in Flood Street, small and rectangular with a window in the narrow end wall, I would lie in bed and watch out for that moment when he would climb up the drainpipe and knock on my window to let him in. For there was no doubt in my mind that he would do that. I didn't know exactly where Germany was or how long it might take a man to travel from Germany to Flood Street, but it seemed unlikely, impossible even, that our father would just leave and never come back to see us. He had not died. He had escaped death, for sure, and would be walking back to London to make his home with us.

So far, then, my young life, for all that it was absurdly
privileged in many respects, nevertheless featured the same
kind of grieving and wishing and and if only . . . that
thousands of other boys and girls were going through
at that time. Some resources - the power to choose, the
authority to make things happen our way, the vision of a
future - we simply didn't have, and such constructs were
never, I think, reflected in our language. Frustratingly,
my own language didn't reflect much at the best of times
because I had developed a bad stammer. It was all I could
do get my name out. I would get stuck on some consonant
or other and then typically there would be a long pause
while I tried to unblock the sticking point and coax the
word out of my mouth. "Take your time," the old man
would say kindly. "We're not in a hurry."

2

SCHOOL

Gibbs was classified as a pre-preparatory school. It was a day school for boys aged between 5 and 8, and turned out to be an altogether better school for me than Mitford Colmer had been. It bestowed the exclusive right to wear the school uniform, a maroon blazer and a floppy maroon cap. It meant no girls, it meant football once a week, mince for lunch and proper classrooms with proper teachers. It meant double desks and sharing, but that was all right. We could talk and smuggle sweets into the classroom. Pretty young women in twin-sets taught us things; sometimes they were so pretty that our hearts would swoon and we would fall in love. In imagination I would win my teacher's heart by a fearless exhibition of flying round the room, swooping over the heads of the entire dining hall while the boys and teachers were eating their cottage pie. One day, maybe in my second year at Gibbs, maybe when I was six and a half, some sort of psycho-sexual frenzy possessed our entire class. Our pretty teacher had set us some work, excused herself and left the room. We waited for the best part of three minutes and when she didn't come back we scrambled out of the room to find her, to see if she was in the loo, and what she might be up to. Maybe some of us were just easily led, others clearly didn't know where they were going or why they were doing this. Seconds later - it seemed - the smooth be-suited headmaster, Michael Holding, was standing on the stairs telling us to come down in single file each with our left hand outstretched towards him. One stroke of the ruler each. A couple of boys cried.

Some crazy things were provided for the boys and we accepted most of them as entirely reasonable. A barrel chested man in his forties, stripped to his vest, would hand out boxing gloves to his class. He would then sit on a hard-backed chair at one end of the room where this "PE" lesson was taking place, and tell us to get in line at the other. One by one we were directed to run at this man as fast as we could and hit him in the chest with a punch hard enough, he instructed us, to knock him off his chair. We had music lessons too where we sang folksongs. The tunes were fun, but the lyrics were baffling:

"Weel may the keel row, the keel row, the keel row

Weel may the keel row that my wee laddie's in"

Few, if any, of us had the foggiest idea what was going on here.

"Dashing away with the smoothing iron" seemed bizarre if not comical, while

"Oh don't deceive me, Oh never leave me,

How could you use a poor maiden so?" always sounded dodgy and unappealing.

We had school holidays, of course, and mine were almost always spent at Linkenholt with Nanny and Robert. During the time between my first year at Gibbs as a five-year-old and leaving the school at eight I got much closer to my grandfather Roland Dudley and grandmother

Mabel. Close enough, at any rate, to become familiar with some of their little ways. Grandpop, as Robert and I called him, was a large man, sturdily built, who had come back to England from India where he had spent the best part of his career working as a civil engineer for the British government. He had been an outstanding mathematician at his grammar school in Wellingborough and passed what he referred to as "the Admiralty Exams" with distinction, so a posting to India in the engineering division of the civil service was, as he saw it, a just and fair progression - and apt recognition of his abilities. He was perfectly happy and fulfilled in India: there were challenging projects in the work itself, there was the Club, the comradeship, bridge and duck shoots, and very soon he was in a position to send back to Wellingborough for Mabel, his childhood sweetheart, to sort out some suitable clothes, get herself onto the next packet ship and to come out to marry and live with him.

When he was 45, Roland returned to England with Mabel and their two children and enough money to buy a manor house with a 700-acre farm and the village that went with it. This was Linkenholt. Roland had been dabbling in the property market. He partly owned a steel foundry in south east London and although he now possessed a huge chunk of prime arable land he wasn't remotely interested in agriculture: he had bought the land for the shooting - then, as now, one of the finest partridge and pheasant shoots in Hampshire. Nevertheless, Roland would keep a watchful, if untutored eye on the day-to-day iterations of farm work and soon started asking why modern machinery wasn't being used to accelerate some of the basic processes - like ploughing, for instance. His tenant farmer explained to him that horses and their manure formed the basis of good practice in agriculture: horses were necessary and precious assets, the *sine qua non* of a decently run farm. Grandpop would have none of this nonsense.

He dismissed the tenant, brought the first caterpillar tractor to England and a combine harvester to follow. Next he set about inventing: first an enormous Heath-Robinson style contraption for drying grass and then an even bigger, even more complex mechanism involving belts, wheels and pulleys for drying the harvested corn to reduce its moisture content and increase its storage life. Both systems would result in the farmer being able to sell product to the market later than others could, and thereby at a more favourable price. In addition, he could do what he wanted with the 700 acres now under his control: he began to think about enhancing the shoot by planting such crops and woodland in strategic parts of the estate as would give appropriate cover for his young birds.

He was a Tory and a radical with little innate respect for tradition. Far from being daunted by the mockery, the sneery disdain, the many taunts that had come his way from the nation's farming community to whom the very idea of mechanisation was anathema, he felt energised, even inspired. He was fond of greengages and wanted to grow a greengage tree in his garden, maybe an espalier here along one of the garden walls. Can't be done, said local experts. Soil's not right, wall's facing the wrong direction, you'll never do it. He took the necessary corrective action, no doubt using plenty of bagged chemicals, and he did it. Stubborn? Obstinate? Yes, of course - but the greengages were sweet and plentiful and Roland's cussed determination had demonstrated one of his defining characteristics.

Roland - otherwise Grandpop

When Michael was killed and the war ended Roland was sixty-five - and a hero. Farm machinery had helped with the country's food production during the war; Roland had served on the government's War Agricultural Committee; he had done a stint as High Sheriff of Hampshire. Yet he didn't make it easy for others to get along with him: he didn't do upper-class charm and he had none of the smoothness of a landed aristo. He was what I think of now as a blunt country landowner who aligned himself unequivocally with the kind of reasoning, testing and proof which the sciences provide; he held a deep distrust of the arts alongside a wistful longing for the return of

Marie Lloyd, the double-entendre and the music hall; he was a kind man, ambitious for his family, with strongly-held views typical of the Conservative entrepreneur that he was. The idea of the State interfering in anything at all in peacetime made him angry. He could never bring himself to forgive Herbert Morrison for imposing some terrible constraint or other - as he saw it - on "poor hardworking people" like himself.

He was a rich man when I first became aware of him as my grandfather. Throughout his sixties and seventies, he would shuffle off after breakfast to his large office on one side of the house. Here he would spend most of the morning on farm and other business, mostly, I suspect, in consultation with his farm manager and the farm accountant. Until I was six - and Grandpop was sixty-six - Robert and I would spend most days with Nanny, but as we developed more and more awareness of who was who and what was what and how we should behave in the big house, we were able to give Nanny more and more time to herself while we went off to find our grandmother.

Mabel Dudley, Granny to us, was a cosy woman, warm, considerate and utterly wonderful with people. She managed the large house with its cook, its butler, and other helping staff without show but with effortless skill and attention to detail. As a result, she was greatly liked and respected by everyone who worked at Linkenholt. The house was usually full of flowers from the garden: the ground floor gave off a distinctive smell of beeswax furniture polish mingling with stocks, chrysanthemums or whatever was in season. Acute arthritis gave her constant pain, yet she found the energy to take up her stick and walk with us into the garden and round the large cedar tree to the vegetable garden which was her special delight.

Mabel - otherwise 'Granny'

Here Tom, the head gardener, would welcome her with pleasant chat and share his ideas about cropping and staffing and pricing . . . for this was no mere vegetable patch for house consumption only, this was a full scale market garden. Every Tuesday Tom would fill his van with produce from Mrs. Dudley's garden (as it was known) and drive the nine miles or so to Andover. Here, in the central shopping square, he would park up outside Reg Burden's shop selling fresh fish and vegetables. There would be discussion, money would change hands, Tom would have a cup of tea with Reg and then he'd unload the agreed amounts of fruit and veg and drive back to Linkenholt. I know all this because much later, when I was about twelve, I would go with him.

On Fridays Granny would go to Andover to buy her fish from Reg Burden. Douglas, the chauffeur, would have washed and polished the Bentley for us and when we arrived at the fish shop we were greeted royally. Mr. Burden - she would never call him "Reg" - was at his most gracious when talking to Granny. He would tell her about the various fish which were lying in crushed ice on his sloping display and she would make her choice. Then - and this for me was always the high spot of our visit - Mr. Burden would take our fishes over to his bench at the side of the shop. Once there he would take a sharp knife and set about preparing them: gutting, maybe scaling, maybe filleting. Having got them ready he would come back to talk some more to Granny while he washed them carefully in a bucket of fresh water. I found the whole preparation process so deliciously yucky, and sensuous and fascinating: Mr. Burden with his sleeves rolled up, splashing fishy water all over his long apron, drops of water stuck to the hairs on his forearms, the palms of his hands sliding all over the slithery fish, the rough throwaway gesture involved in getting them back onto his bench and wrapping them first in shiny fresh brown paper and then in an old copy of Reynolds News or the Daily Express. I found myself thinking about this process long after we had got home to Linkenholt, how luscious and naughty and utterly desirable it seemed. I wondered how old I would have to be before I dared ask Mr. Burden whether he would let me have a go.

I turned eight in 1949, in what was my last year at Gibbs. This was the year in which Miss Harvey became our class teacher. There was some shuffling around of seating positions in our new classroom and I found myself sharing a double desk with a little boy - shorter than me by a couple of inches - with whom I had exchanged grunts of greeting and recognition, but that was about all. I hadn't given him much thought until we started sharing a desk: he had always appeared a bit slow - maybe he spoke quite slowly. He wasn't particularly athletic - I can't remember him playing football with us for instance, but he probably did. Like me he had put up with the familiar smell of stale cottage pie in the dining hall; like me he had piped out "Johnny's So Long at the Fair". No doubt we had both gagged on the puke-inducing scent of warm milk, well on its way to going off. We were comparatively old hands at Gibbs and yet there was something very special to come, something we could neither of us have imagined. The genius of Miss Harvey.

Miss Harvey was an older woman with standard-issue spectacles and short grey hair, some of which she swept back into a clip behind her head. She was an astonishingly gifted teacher of seven- and eight- year olds. Every lesson with her was a joy, everything from learning our times-tables to listening to Greek myths. I still remember her account of the seventeen-year old Theseus getting up early, washing and going out to see if this would be the day he could get that mighty boulder to budge . . . . . She read us wonderful stories from the classics; she showed us paintings and talked about them; she taught us a bit of basic Latin. I think my desk-mate, indeed I think everyone in the class, enjoyed Miss Harvey's lessons. One day, this same desk-mate told me that his grandmother had asked him to bring a little friend to stay when he went there for his annual summer visit. He said "Would I like to be his friend and go and stay with him at his grandparents' home in Kent this coming August?"

Stay? . . . on my own? I hardly knew the boy and certainly not as a friend, but, come to think of it, I hardly knew anyone as a friend. There was my family, of course, but my family was getting a bit splintered. My mother had re-married in 1947 - when I was six - and she was more or less preoccupied getting to know Richard, her new husband. During term-time we all lived in Flood Street, and of course Robert and Nanny were there too. We three - Robert, Nanny and I - were a happy unit together, so much so that, rather than leave us on our own when it came to be her notional "day off" Nanny would very often take us to the Serpentine or to a boating pond in Regents Park and then, joy of joys, we would sometimes stop off at an expensive looking tea room in Sloane Street. Here Nanny would order a pot of tea for herself and scoops of strawberry and vanilla ice cream in a metal dish for Robert and me. Maybe she had our ration books as well as her own. Sometimes, but not very often, cousins or the children of our mother's friends might come round, but I didn't have any close friends from school whom I might have invited home for tea or anything like that. There were birthday parties, of course, but they were a different matter. Altogether different. You didn't have to be a friend to go to someone's birthday party. Someone, usually in your class at school would ask you and you'd go. You didn't have to be their friend.

In the school holidays Robert, Nanny and I would stay at Linkenholt. This was feeling very much like a proper home to me: I had lived there for the first four years of my life and I loved it. What was there not to love? Nanny was there to care for us and, as Robert and I got older Granny wanted us down to spend more time with her in the drawing room and in the library, which meant less time in the nursery upstairs with Nanny. There was masses of space outside and on fine days we were encouraged to go out, explore and play: soon we could rampage on our bikes across the wild west plains of the front lawn as Wyatt Earp and Billy the Kid or take the bow and arrows made by Douglas for us from the bamboo plants down by the vegetable garden, and stalk pheasants. We hit tennis balls at each other on the tennis court, we built shelters among the laurel scrub which bordered the many pathways in the garden. This was home all right. And we came to realise that, now that our mother had re-married, we were - apart from Granny and Grandpop - the only Dudleys left in the family.

Me and Robert

What exactly did that mean for us? It meant that Grandpop would pay for me and Robert to be educated at Michael's prep school and, God willing - this was one of Grandpop's favourite expressions - at the same public school too; and it meant that we were to spend the lion's share of each school holiday at Linkenholt. It also meant that we would come to know and savour Grandpop's own special world of seed-time and harvest, of fighting the Labour party, of Rudyard Kipling, Robinson Crusoe and Three Old Crows Sat on a Tree. Every day he would expect us to come and have tea with him and Granny in the drawing room: sandwiches and home-made cakes with lemonade for Robert and me and tea for our grandparents. After tea Grandpop would take us round some part of the huge farm with him in his Land Rover, usually because there was something he wanted to check: maybe to do with water levels or game-birds or something esoteric and agricultural that he didn't choose to tell us about. But there was plenty he did want to tell us about, and if being Dudleys meant we were privy to Grandpop's exotic stories about his life in India, maybe in the future it would mean we could learn to shoot pheasants and to drive one of the Land Rovers. Beyond that, we could guess and imagine to our hearts' content, but we knew nothing for certain. The best thing it meant to us in 1949, back at Linkenholt for the Easter holidays, was this: that on Friday afternoon Granny would be going into Andover to get her fish. And after she'd done that she would go, as she always did when we were with her, to the bookshop at the top end of the square and buy us a couple of books each. That's what being part of this funny-old Dudley family meant to us then, not much more and not much less.

If it hadn't been for that invitation Winston might have slipped quietly out of my consciousness and stayed there. As it was, I was finding the idea of going away to stay with his grandparents quite a challenge. It also brought with it a worrying degree of interest, bordering on excitement, from members of my family. It was explained to me several times that this boy Winston was the grandson of Clementine and Winston Churchill. Winston Churchill, I was told for the umpteenth time - as if I might be finding it difficult to understand (like electricity) - had been our Prime Minister and had inspired our fighting men and women, indeed had inspired everybody involved in supporting the war effort, to win a decisive victory in the Second World War, that's the one we've just been fighting. He was the man who had saved this country from Hitler, probably the greatest living Englishman and you're going to stay with him, well fancy that. Nanny told me how Winston Churchill was a truly Great Man, without whose love for his country and inspiring speeches we would not have beaten the Germans. Granny and Grandpop said they were very pleased for me and said they looked forward to hearing all about it. My mother, too, was pleased, but her own mother Olga was overjoyed, and wanted all her rich friends in the South of France to know about it straight away. My Aunt Jane, Granny and Grandpop's only daughter, had spent most of her adult life moving in rather grand circles. She had taken the adage "manners maketh man" to heart. Aunt Jane was most concerned that I should not make a fool of myself with the Churchills, and was generous to a fault (I believed) in offering me advice on my manners - table manners, dress codes, manners to do with standing up and sitting down, talking and not talking, opening and closing doors for people. There seemed to be manners for everything. Her extensive advice on these rather technical matters merely added to the weight of anxiety I was beginning to feel. I was to make sure my hair was tidy, look attentive, smile, be pleasant . . . . . Oh dear, I wasn't sure I'd be able to keep this performance up for long.

Me

Nanny had packed me a small bag of clothes, toothbrush and so on, and on the appointed day in August 1949 Richard took me and my travel bag round to the house where Winston and I were going to be picked up and driven to Chartwell. This was the house where Winston lived with his mother Pamela Churchill. Pamela and Winston's father, Randolph Churchill had divorced in 1946 and not long after that, in 1948, Randolph had got married again to someone called June Osborne. Richard rang the bell, waited for the door to be opened, handed over my suitcase, said "Goodbye, have a good time", and left me to get on with it.

3

AUGUST 1949
(FIRST VISIT)

Someone in a maid's uniform took me up a flight of stairs to a light and spacious drawing room. Mrs. Pamela Churchill, Winston's mother, sat at one end of a long white sofa. She wore a deep blue dress made from a silky material that rustled as she moved. Winston was there too, sitting on the floor, doing something with a comic. He looked exactly the same as he did at school: messy and awkward with his pencil, he made funny noises through his nose when he breathed. His mother was beautiful, really beautiful, calm and poised, smoking a cigarette. "You must be Jonathan" she said. And then, quite shortly after that "The car will be here very soon".

And in minutes, Winston and I were handing our little packed bags over to Penelope who was, she told us, Mrs. Churchill's private secretary. She clearly wasn't going to be driving the big black car - the chauffeur would be doing that - but she would be sitting in the back with us and that would give her a chance to tell us about the arrangements for our visit.

Winston by the car

These, she told us, were perfectly straightforward. "You will not be sleeping in Chartwell itself, but in Orchard Cottage - you know, Winston, that's the one at the bottom of the long sloping orchard at the back of the house. Winston, do you remember Grace Hamblin? Well, she's living there at the moment, and she will make you comfortable, wake you up in the morning and give you your breakfast. You will then have the rest of the morning to yourselves, to play or do whatever you want, but you must be sure to leave time to clean yourselves up and get to Chartwell ready to join the family for lunch at 12.45pm sharp. Has either of you got a watch? Oh, and Mrs. Soames, your Aunt Mary, will be coming over for lunch tomorrow and probably on other days during your visit. Anything you want to ask about any of that?"

I felt it was important to listen carefully to Penelope's talk, even though I didn't know the people or the places she was talking about. When she had finished I went back to my study of the amazing car we were driving in. It was one of those black ministerial-style cars with a partition separating the driver from the passengers in the back. A sliding glass panel was positioned just above seat height on top of the partition so that passengers could, if they wanted to do so, speak to the driver. Just by the handles for opening the rear doors two little seats, one each side, were folded up into the leather fabric covering the robust partition. These were perfect for Winston and me. We could wiggle round, look through the glass panel and watch not only the road, the oncoming traffic, but the dials on the dashboard. And on the speedo - what! - 60 miles per hour! It seemed incredible - it felt as if we were doing about 25 mph, not 60. I had never travelled at 60 mph in my life. This was hugely exciting, and I must have believed that it deserved most, if not all of my attention. I would just stick close to Winston when we got to Chartwell: he would know what the arrangements meant, who everyone was, where to go and what we had to do. I would stick close to him.

Chartwell

My first impressions of Chartwell were dominated by Mrs. Churchill, who exhibited the most delightful open, cheerful and caring disposition in all her dealings, not only with her grandson but with me too. She made it seem as if she had oodles of time for everyone. She appeared to sail through the day with a grace and composure that effectively masked the enormous amount of planning which the running of two very visible households - one here in the Kent countryside, the other in Knightsbridge - entailed. In the summer of 1949 Mr. Churchill was a mere six months away from a general election; he was leader of the Conservative Party in Opposition; he was seventy-four years old, and while the war must have sapped some of his physical strength, his mind was still sharp: he was still a stylish and prolific writer, still a devastating and witty conversationalist, now focused upon winning back the people's mandate and persuading what he still regarded as a fickle electorate that the country desperately needed a Conservative approach to domestic, economic and foreign affairs.

It was difficult for us, for Winston and me, not to get caught up in the excitements involved in preparing for a general election, despite the fact that our life at Chartwell - the comforting and familiar routines of lunch then going for a walk or playing in the garden, then tea, then some reading, then back to Orchard Cottage for bath, a light supper provided by Grace and then bed - was structured to discourage over-stimulated behaviours of any kind. One lunchtime during my first visit we boys were told that there was to be a special event happening in the house that afternoon: Mr. Churchill was going to give a live broadcast to the nation and he was going to deliver his speech into the BBC microphone in his painting studio on the ground floor. If we agreed to be very good indeed, and absolutely silent meaning no sound *at all* we could sit quietly in the studio and watch while he gave the speech. It would be a rousing speech, and we were not to clap or cheer or stamp our feet or anything like that. We were to make no sound *AT ALL*. Was that perfectly understood?

It was. And into Mr. Churchill's painting studio we went. I found it fascinating to watch the process of testing and checking voice levels, trial runs, a red light changing to green and all the paraphernalia of cables and the technology that went with a live broadcast. Mr. Churchill appeared so relaxed, so jolly and chatty before beginning his broadcast, quite undaunted by the prospect of his imminent performance, not nervous at all. And then I found, when the green light went on and he began his speech, that I didn't have the foggiest idea what he was talking about.

The painting studio where the broadcast was taking place was a huge but beautifully proportioned room looking down the garden and across the valley to the woods beyond. Normally this room was out of bounds to us boys, so this was the first time I had been allowed inside the studio. Winston and I were positioned about ten paces away from where Mr. Churchill was sitting in front of the microphone. We were about halfway down the length of the room and on the wall facing us were masses of Mr. Churchill's paintings. At that time Mr. Churchill was still using the room for painting and hanging his finished artworks and now that I had given up listening to the speech he was broadcasting, I became transfixed by the paintings on the wall. It was fun to identify places he had painted in the very gardens here at Chartwell where we had played and mucked about: the swimming pool, the fishpond and the lake in particular. I took a special fancy to his painting of black swans on the lake, and not necessarily for aesthetic reasons. The previous day - I rather shudder to remember this - Winston and I had been stalking the black swans to see how close we could get to them without getting our feet wet when Winston announced he needed to do a poo. Rather than trek back to Orchard Cottage he reckoned that the reeds and bulrushes where we were stalking would provide adequate screening from the house, that he was going to use leaves for loo paper and do a poo right there by the lakeside. I was to keep lookout and let him know if anyone was coming. Not much fun for me, really - my genteel upbringing hadn't prepared me for pooing *al fresco* among bulrushes, so I felt rather left out of whatever fun Winston might be having. But that was the kind of child I was: a bit anxious perhaps, a bit conformist, and woefully out of touch with my wild, adventurous side. I was much more comfortable when Winston agreed to play sporty games - like catching tennis balls or playing french cricket or croquet etc - than when he regressed, as was his custom, to being a daredevil or playing the fool.

We may have been only eight years old, but sometimes it seemed to me that Winston's curious sense of "fun" exceeded the limits of acceptable good taste. Someone had given us a long metal tube to play with, a real and rather battered army periscope. Frankly we hadn't been making much use of it - there were only so many times we found it engaging to stick the periscope out from behind a tree or round a corner of the house to peep out without being detected. On this particular day Winston had the idea of standing in the flower beds just beneath the ground-floor windows and sticking the end of the periscope up against window panes to check what was going on inside. No one in the rooms would know they were being watched. Ha-ha-ha. Only what Winston really had in mind was standing just below his grandmother's bathroom window and peeping in while she was having a bath.

Not at all a good idea, I told him, but Winston wouldn't listen to my objections. I removed myself from what I knew was going to develop into a crime scene, and watched what happened from the comparative safety of the lawn. Sure enough, Winston didn't manage too well with the Keeping Quiet side of his task. He crashed into the buddleia growing in the flower bed under the bathroom window and then tramped his way noisily through the dahlias to get himself in a good position. The end of the periscope got caught in the belt of his short trousers, and when he yanked it free it hit against the window pane with a sharp clatter loud enough to make Mrs. Churchill jump out of her bath - if she had been in it, that is.

I never found out whether she was in the bath or even whether she had been in the bathroom at the time.

What I do know is that Mrs. Churchill presently came out of the front door and took Winston away for a little chat. He was quite red in the face when he re-joined me in the garden, but would say nothing about what had happened. He didn't have the periscope with him. That had clearly been confiscated and we never saw it again.

I suspect that Mrs. Churchill had passed it on to Eddie, Mr. Churchill's bodyguard, who had probably given it to us to play with in the first place. Eddie had his own room in the big house, and although we didn't see very much of him, we got on very well. His title "bodyguard" sounded dangerous and exotic and we did our best to get him to tell us about his life as a bodyguard and what he would do if he discovered a Nazi hiding in the bushes by the front of the house, waiting for Mr. Churchill to come out so he could do him in. Eddie gave all sorts of elaborate and funny answers to our questions and we were never quite sure how much of what he said was true in real life and how much he was making up. But it was beguiling stuff - Eddie was a great story-teller. I was quite in awe of him, especially when we nearly discovered where he kept his pistol. We had been egging him on to back up his stories of shooting and killing with hard evidence: where was his gun now, for instance? Was it a pistol? "Oh, now, listen," he said, "I can't go around telling people where I keep things like that, can I? Suppose I told you where I keep my pistols - imagine the situation if you were approached by a spy of one sort or another and he promised to give you bags and bags of chocolates and jelly-babies in return for you telling him about my guns - I mean, well, if it was a good offer, you'd be tempted, wouldn't you? And where would that leave me? I'd be well and truly up a gum tree . . . . "But we weren't happy with that. We started looking. He didn't seem to mind us lifting corners of his rug, moving his books and cushions, peering under his wardrobe, feeling behind the radiator. It was only when we turned our attention to the bed, that his entire countenance changed. "Stop that right away!" he ordered, and the command came from a place in his character that we hadn't heard before. He was deadly serious. When he spoke next he was more like the Eddie we knew: "Now, boys, I've got work to do, so you'd better be off. And mind you keep away from those pesky spies with their bags of sweets."

We went round to the back of the house, en route to the swimming pool. On the way we walked along a path bordered by narrow flower beds, each of which was resplendent with plants I had never seen before, plants we didn't have at Linkenholt. The plants were tall, each one a different colour, and each one showing an abundance of trumpet-shaped flowers. They had a strong, enticing scent and Winston told me that these were tobacco plants, proper name Nicotiana. He told me his great secret about them too: you pluck off a flower and put the pointed end of the trumpet in your mouth and when you suck you get a shot of the most delicious honey-sweet syrup. This was a puzzling thing indeed: how could a flower as sweet and delicious as this have any connection with the manky, bitter smell of nicotine-infected tobacco smoke? I thought there was probably quite an obvious explanation so I didn't mention it to anyone.

Figs, too, were a bit special. There was a fig tree espaliered against one section of the south facing wall which was now covered with strange-looking fruit, dark purple-black, sitting heavily on the branches. I had never seen a fig before let alone eaten one - again, we didn't have a fig tree at Linkenholt - but June Spencer-Churchill, Randolph's new wife, saw me looking at them oddly and picked one off.

"Try it", she said. "What do you do?" I asked her. "You put it in your mouth and you eat it", she replied - as if I was a bit simple. I had been worrying, I suppose, about my Aunt Jane's etiquette lessons and the correct knives and forks and can you use your fingers and all that carry-on. But here we were in the garden, stuffing figs into our mouths and it felt a bit wicked . . .well, it felt brilliant!

June Spencer-Churchill

Mr. and Mrs. Winston Churchill had three grown-up daughters: Diana, the eldest, lived in London with her husband, the Conservative MP Duncan Sandys and their three children; Sarah, whom I never met, was an actress who spent quite a lot of time in America; and Mary who lived in Chartwell Farm House, right next to Chartwell itself, with her husband Nicholas Soames who was also a Conservative MP. Mary Soames used to come up to Chartwell regularly to spend time with her mother - she would very often be there for lunch while Winston and I were there. Her first child, also called Nicholas, had been born in February 1948, just eighteen months before our visit.

Randolph was Mr. and Mrs. Churchill's only son, and
Winston's dad. Yet it was a complete surprise to me that
Randolph and June should appear at Chartwell when
they did - in some ways an unwarranted surprise because
this was their family and it was none of my business if
they should decide to turn up and stay. What I found
curious about them being here was that no one had talked
openly about the fact that they were coming. Winston
had mentioned nothing, but maybe he didn't know about
it. There had been no mention of Randolph and June
arriving among the family at lunchtime when I would
certainly have heard it. This still strikes me as a bit peculiar
since June was over six months pregnant. Maybe they had
telephoned to say they were coming at very short notice.
As I say, it was none of my business.

One of the high spots of that first visit to Chartwell was
meeting Randolph for the first time. Probably the most
unusual encounter of my young life up to that point. It was
a hot day and Winston and I were messing about in the
swimming pool as we often did when suddenly there was a
mighty roar from the direction of the house. I looked up to
see what was going on and there was a large fat man with
very little on, clutching his stomach, running at us as fast
as he could in a fearsome charge and roaring at the top of
his voice. Reaching the edge of the pool he flung himself
horizontally on to the water and as he took off, let go of the
swimming pants he'd been clutching. As he stretched out his
arms on the dive, the swimming pants dropped down his
legs to his ankles and off into the pool. There he was, stark
naked, flopping about in the water, clearly enjoying himself.
It was a disturbing moment for me: an extremely large
naked man with lots of hair and a voice well marinaded in
years of whisky and cigarettes to give it a distinctly booming
quality. Disturbing? Well, yes - disturbing.

Randolph

"This is Jonathan, Randolph." Mary Soames pointed in my direction and he nodded at me. That was as official as our introduction was going to get. He waded over to talk to Winston while somebody on the pool's edge - maybe June - managed to fish the over-sized swimming trunks from the water, and ring them out. Someone else, probably one of the housemaids, took a few steps from the house with towels for Randolph, who was busy drying himself with my towel and with Winston's. The housemaid kept her eyes suitably averted and left the new towels with June before retreating to the safety of indoors.

The next day I went up the garden with Winston to say goodbye to Randolph and June. Randolph was wearing battledress, a lightweight camouflage affair. I had no idea why this should be - and I don't believe Winston did either. He didn't make a fuss about saying goodbye to his father. Maybe there was a brief hug and a kiss and then he just carried on with whatever he had been doing earlier. I never saw Randolph again at Chartwell.

On good days Winston and I played in the swimming pool, or maybe we went for a walk with Winston's Aunt Mary or Aunt Diana and Winston's cousins, or maybe we were taken out in the car to visit friends or family of Mr. Churchill. But throughout our time together Winston and I never managed to generate an easy or an open style of chat together.

It was strange. He clearly didn't have a great number of pals where he lived with his mother and neither did I. Apart from being basically friendless, it turned out that we really didn't have much in common. I loved sporty things, especially ball games, Winston not. Winston liked poring over comics or using crayons to draw on a large exercise pad, or making shapes and patterns with coloured paper, a pair of scissors and some glue - not my sort of thing at all. In the chats I do remember us having, usually at night in our beds in Orchard Cottage, Winston would do his best to irritate me with his two favourite topics of conversation - if you can call what usually happened "conversation". The first started off with him reminding me that I was only a guest here and furthermore, only a guest here because he had managed to get me invited in the first place; the second turned into rather a one-sided competition and required us to score points: whose family had more money, history, success, fame, land etcetera - his or mine. Neither topic brought us closer together. I didn't particularly mind that our relationship was a bit strained because I really was having a good time at Chartwell, and didn't feel at all dependent on Winston for that. Our relationship may have been strained, but at least it was a relationship which brought me into contact with some interesting people and took me to some exciting places. So I just got on with it and tried not to dwell on his reluctance to trust me or to talk openly with me. But it was difficult.

Sometimes Winston didn't share information that he had been given to pass on to me. Like a change in the lunch arrangements, or when his father and June would be coming to stay, or who the guests at lunch were going to be. That kind of thing was annoying. Winston's noisy breathing and snuffling were annoying too, but then I discovered what a debilitating affliction it was to have asthma and I forgave him that. But I'm sure he found me equally, if not more, annoying: after all I was limiting the time he could spend being loved and possibly spoilt by his grandmother and by his grandfather. I wasn't aware of Winston popping into the big house on his own to spend time with either of them - for the most part he and I stuck together and whatever I was doing, he would probably be doing it too. So I was more than surprised one evening when, during one of our chats just before lights out, Winston said "My grandfather has bought me a small version of a petrol-engine motor car for my 9th birthday". My first thought was "You're lying!" My second was "When the heck did you hear this bit of stupendous news - because you've scarcely been out of my sight all day?" but I said, "That's amazing - when can we go and see it?" and he said, "It's at Biggin Hill Airport and they're getting it ready for me. My grandfather is going to take me over to the airport for a practice drive in it after you've gone home."

I think he really was lying. I think he must have invented the story about the car in the belief that I would somehow feel put in my place by it, or envious or something like that. I never worked out why he should want me to feel bad - maybe he was the tiniest bit jealous of me. There seemed to be not the slightest justification for that. OK, I did seem to get on well with all the Churchill relations who popped in to Chartwell for the occasional lunch or dinner. But it was particularly disappointing to me that, when we were alone, Winston would play stupid power games and do his best to discomfort me.

When we were with other people he gave no sign that we were anything but the best of friends. The time we were most visible to family and guests was during the hallowed ritual of lunch - or, as I rather think Mrs. Churchill called it, luncheon. Every day at 12.45 the family and anyone else who had been invited for lunch would meet for drinks upstairs on the spacious landing outside the dining room on the first floor. Several chairs had been placed here and among them stood a drinks trolley with ice bucket, glasses and all manner of alcoholic drinks, chasers, nuts and nibbles and - and this was the great thrill of it for me - a large glass jug of tomato juice. I had never tasted tomato juice before, and it immediately became my favourite drink of all time. Winston and I only managed to drink one glass before Mrs. Churchill encouraged us to put our empty glasses back on the trolley and make our way into the dining room. Here was a room full of natural daylight: two large sash windows looked out across the drive and the front lawn. Along the centre of the room stood a beautiful dining table, shining with beeswax polish and designed to accommodate up to ten people in comfort. Laid for lunch the table looked utterly beguiling with shiny silver cutlery and, placed in groups around the middle sections, sets of the most exquisite silver pieces, most of which were designed to carry salt, pepper and mustard. I had seen silver cruets before, because we had them at Linkenholt, but I had never seen anything like the other pieces: here silver had been crafted to produce silver game birds in different poses - pheasants, for one, with extravagant tail plumage - and such lovely creatures seemed rather out of place with anything so utilitarian as salt and mustard pots. Also on the table with these gorgeous things was another silver piece that was completely new to me. This was a small vase-shaped object, filled not with flowers but with little spears, made of feather stems, sharpened at the point like quills. After a bit, as course followed course and meal followed meal, it became clear what these little sharp points were provided for.

If it was to be a family-only lunch, Mr. Churchill would arrive from the direction of his bedroom on the first floor. He would have been working in bed for most of the morning, reading or dictating to his private secretary. Mr. Churchill's rooms on the first floor were, of course very much out of bounds to the boys. On such days as these he would arrive for lunch wearing his navy blue boiler suit and a pair of the most exquisite velvet bedroom slippers, a deep navy colour with large capital initials WSC intertwined on the uppers in gorgeous gold embroidery. He sometimes wore a cream silk scarf loosely tied around his neck. He would take a large glass of whisky and put quite a lot of soda water on top of it. He would take a sip of his drink, look round approvingly at the members of his beloved family assembled there and, with a big smile on his face, begin to talk. This was his family. He was at home.

One day at Chartwell we were having lunch, as usual, in the dining room. When lunch was finished Mr. Churchill looked over to where I was sitting from his place at the head of the long dining table. He said, "Come here, Jonathan, come and stand by my chair." It was 1949 and I was eight and a half. He was seventy-four. I got up and went round the table to stand by the old man's chair on his left side. He turned and looked kindly at me with what I took to be almost a twinkle. "What are you going to do with yourself when you grow up?" I didn't say anything straight away. It seemed quite a difficult question for me to answer.

The words were clear and I understood perfectly well what Mr. Churchill meant. I would do my best to give an answer even though I didn't have much of a sense of career options, didn't feel nearly powerful enough to set about choosing things, anything at all really. What are you going to do when you grow up? How on earth would I know? I was eight and looking into the future seemed an utterly pointless exercise.

At my age, it seemed to me, it was important to get on with it, whatever it was, as well as I could. Making the best of whatever cropped up, or whatever was provided. In return, as it were, I would do what I was told and make myself as agreeable as possible to grown-ups by being polite, useful perhaps - that sort of thing. Just get on with it and leave thinking about the future to others. I didn't say any of this to Mr. Churchill. Indeed, I still didn't say anything at all, and I could sense, as I stood feebly by Mr. Churchill's chair, that my inability to answer his straightforward question was beginning to worry the other members of the family who were sitting round the lunch table.

I didn't have a good answer ready, but I knew I had to say something. The question had rendered me so speechless that after a bit the silence got to be embarrassing for everyone who was there. It had gone on too long - now it was unacceptable. Luckily it was a family day, nobody except Winston, his aunt Mary Soames, his grandmother and grandfather and I were there for lunch. But I rather think I heard mutterings from the far end of the table, Mrs. Churchill and Mrs. Soames urging Mr. Churchill to leave me alone, let the boy go, move on, don't put him through this torture, why don't we all go for a walk . . . . . and so on.

But I still stood there, my face contorted, lips puckered and locked together in a ghastly trembling as I tried to force some words out. Mr. Churchill kept his eyes on my face, his expression kind and sympathetic. "Take your time," he said, "we're not in a hurry". For my part I wanted neither his kindness nor his sympathy. I just wanted to hear my voice say something, for my words to bludgeon their way through the barricades of barbed wire in my mouth and fire off into the room.

My mouth relaxed enough for me to speak, and I felt the words coming. I had got stuck on the first big consonant, an "F", and I wonder now whether Mr. Churchill was expecting me to say "Foreign Secretary", "Film Director" or something a bit distinctively outrageous, like "Philanderer". When the words came I said "Fishmonger. I'd like to be a fishmonger when I grow up." "Fishmonger, eh?" he echoed. "Well, well". I lifted my eyes from the carpet and looked into Mr. Churchill's face as he registered the hopelessly inadequate character of my reply. Gone was the sympathy, the kindly and supportive attention which the stuck "F" had elicited. In its place was a deep boredom, an ennui so implacable there was nothing for it but to retreat to my chair and hope that I would never have to speak again. I had, it seemed to me, not only given a foolish answer in a botched and inelegant fashion, I had offended against a set of expectations which - well - I had intimations about but didn't fully understand. Maybe I could have said "Farmer". But that was Grandpop's life after all - it wasn't necessarily going to be right for me. Maybe I should have told the truth: "What do I want to be? Crikey, Mr. Churchill, how should I know?" But that, for all that it was the truth, would probably have sounded cocky or pretentious or, more likely, downright rude.

No, my answer constituted an offence against what Granny and Grandpop's daughter, my Aunt Jane, would have regarded as the proper way to behave, and I felt like a complete idiot. I remembered being puzzled about why Aunt Jane would never refer to Reg Burden as "Reg" or as "Mr. Burden" but always as "Burden", as if the poor man wasn't quite acceptable in the world of polite society. Maybe this had something to do with it. She had made clear what she expected from me in terms of polite behaviour: I was to open doors for grown-ups and stand up immediately whenever a lady came into the room. I was to call men of her social class who were over the age of twenty-five-or-so "Sir", and rather than initiate conversation with a grown-up I was to wait until somebody spoke to me first. Perhaps if we had got on to careers and career prospects she could have saved me from going off the rails in my first few days at Chartwell.

Often Mr. and Mrs. Churchill would have guests for lunch, sometimes senior members of the Conservative party (maybe Anthony Eden or RAB Butler), sometimes politicians or intellectuals from Commonwealth countries (I remember Robert Menzies the Australian prime minister and his wife) and sometimes members of the family - like Randolph and June, or Christopher and Mary Soames or Diana Sandys and one or more of her three children. It did not seem to matter who was coming, Winston and I were always expected to join the party. I remember Mr. Menzies' visit in particular because, to my great surprise, I was seated next to him. We were having roast grouse for lunch - today was was August 13th and much was made of the fact that our main course had been shot by friends of the Churchill's the previous day on some moor in Yorkshire. Mr. Menzies clearly enjoyed celebrating the traditions associated with the the beginning of the grouse season as the adults toasted the resolve of the courier who had driven through the night to bring these birds to Chartwell from the very first shoot of the season.

Grouse was a whole new experience for me and a baffling one. The birds were served as they were cooked, in one piece - in other words you weren't expected to take a slice or two of the breast or thigh of one of the birds as they were brought round on a serving platter, oh no: you were expected to take the whole bird onto your plate, carve it up for yourself and eat it. I was having quite a few problems with this novel way of having the food served, and now Mr. Menzies really came into his own. He noticed that I was wriggling in a bog of ignorance and self-doubt, and immediately set about helping me to cope with the dismantling of the whole roast bird sitting on my plate. He started by telling me about the way a grouse's bones were put together, pointing out key bone joints to look for and developed the biology lesson into a short practical session on carving. "Get the knife at such an angle, like so, and press it against the breast bone here. Can you do that? No, don't use so much force - you'll slosh the gravy onto my trousers as well as yours if you lean on it like that." Mr. Menzies was a great sport and I felt I was on sufficiently good terms with him to confess that I didn't like the taste of the grouse at all. It reminded me of something unpleasant I had tasted at the dentists, but I couldn't remember what. "A bad tooth?" he suggested. "Ever had really bad toothache?" he asked. But I didn't think I had. "Don't make yourself eat any more", he said, "you've had enough. And look, they've started to clear away the plates". So saying, he stretched across me to help himself to one of the little quills from the silver spear-carrier just in front of me.

What followed was an episode of social etiquette that

would have amazed and confounded Aunt Jane. I couldn't wait to tell her about it. The grown-ups would, when their plate had been cleared away, take one of the feather-quill toothpicks and with a great display of studied elegance, pick their teeth. (Well, all right then - *almost* all the grown-ups.) One hand held the toothpick and got started on the serious business of dental hygiene while the other hand cupped in front of the mouth prevented anyone seeing details of the prodding and poking going on inside. There was a question of style associated with the action of masking your mouth: smokers usually got it at once and displayed just the right amount of decorous chic with the cupped hand; people with stubby fingers or, worse, bitten fingernails, struggled. Tooth-picking time was, on the whole, quiet time - like being at the dentist, after all. Not an ideal moment for deep and meaningful conversation. I thought Aunt Jane would be a natural for these tooth-picking interludes: she was a smoker with elegant hands who would never opt for the deep and meaningful if there was a bit of quiet time on offer.

I forget who the visitors were on the day we had caviar for lunch, but they would have been special. I suspect some of them would have been Americans, maybe Mr. Harriman or Mr. Truman, because Mr. Churchill introduced the starter to the assembled guests with unusual brio. "The caviar you have in front of you", he announced, "was sent as a gift to Clemmie and me by Joseph Stalin. He says it is the finest caviar in the world. I would like to tell him that we agree with him, but we will taste it first. Whether it is the finest in the world or not, I am confident that we will enjoy it". Well - it tasted very salty and very fishy to me, but that wasn't really the point. More extravagant and more wonderful than the large, black, blueberry-sized eggs I would get to in a minute was the marble pot in which they were presented. My pot on its own would have made an exceptional present. The pot had a lid, of course, which had been sealed during its journey from Russia; it was the shape and size of a large dish of shaving soap and it was the colour of pale stone, probably fashioned from some kind of smooth marble material, porphyry perhaps or onyx, or something else from the limestone family. And there were enough of these lovely pots for everyone at lunch to have one.

On those days when visitors came for lunch Mr. Churchill would dress in what I took to be a very formal costume. During my ten-day visit that year I only remember seeing Mr. Churchill wear three outfits: there was the boiler suit and slippers that he would put on when no one but family was around - and that included any of his children and their partners or his grandchildren and their friends; there was what I have just called that 'very formal costume', a version of old-fashioned parliamentary pinstriped-trousers, black jacket with waistcoat, and, in his case, a white shirt sporting a wing collar and bow tie; and there was the gorgeous black velvet smoking jacket that he would sometimes wear in the evening, with orthodox black DJ trousers and those amazing embroidered house slippers. He was wearing his boiler suit for lunch on the day that his eldest daughter Diana Sandys brought two of her three children to the house for lunch. Mary Soames was there too, because I remember us all going on a tremendously lively walk after lunch. Diana Sandys and Mary Soames took us down across the parkland on the other side of the lake, and around the cleared path through the woods. The grown-up sisters were chatting away to each other, while we four children scampered about together, or just walked and talked. The memory of that walk can still generate in me a curious kind of joy: I found myself becoming bewitched by Edwina Sandys, by her style, her look, her very strangeness. Edwina was nearly eleven, and it surprised me to be feeling this way. After all it wasn't as if this was the first time I had ever spent time with girls my own age. Aunt Jane had two daughters, one a bit older than me the other a bit younger, and Robert and I would sometimes find ourselves at Linkenholt when Aunt Jane and her daughters were staying there too. And occasionally we would meet up with them in London, for our respective Nannies got on well, and they lived not far away from us in Chelsea. But Edwina fascinated me in a way that neither of my cousins did. Of course I didn't mention this strange attraction that I had felt to anyone - not to Winston (obviously) nor, when I got home, to Rob, Nanny, my mother, nor to anyone else at all.

Mr. Churchill most certainly wore the very formal dress on the day he took us in the car to Chequers.

He didn't do the driving himself but the same nice chauffeur who had driven Winston, Penelope and me to Chartwell on that very first day of my visit opened the back door of the same big sedan car for Mr. Churchill. After he was comfortably seated and his Personal Private Secretary had gone round to the other side of the car and got in next to him Winston and I clambered in and sat on our little seats behind the driver's partition. Chequers is the official country house of whoever is the British Prime Minister at the time. Of course Mr. Churchill was not Prime Minister then: that was Clement Attlee, leader of the Labour Party. I think Mr. Churchill must have been going to visit Mr. Attlee on some sort of official business, or maybe this was some kind of informal, maybe comradely, invitation that Mr. Attlee had sent to the Leader of the Opposition. Nevertheless, I secretly

wondered how friendly the encounter between these
men would turn out to be since a massively important
general election was scheduled to take place in the
following February - Mr. Churchill's wireless broadcast
to the nation on the Home Service had alerted me to the
desperate immediacy of this contest.

Mr. Churchill at Chartwell

Four years earlier in 1945, the Labour Party had famously won the first general election after the war. I was four, and living in Flood Street with my mother, Nanny and Robert. Nanny had been listening to the early morning news and I went with her as she took a cup of tea to my mother in bed. She said to my mother "Labour's in" - two little words which have stuck with me for all that they meant very little to me when she said them. At various times over the next four years, my grandfather and Aunt Jane would parade their own Conservative values and prejudices to me with such insistence that I began to think of Labour as my enemy rather than my friend, as a force to be feared and hated rather than respected and admired. And so it had taken the shortest of short steps for me to reach the conclusion that the leader of this Labour Party must be an extremely bad man indeed. I fancied he must look like some sort of ogre, with an evil-looking face, black teeth perhaps, and squinty eyes. This was the very man, this Mr. Attlee, that we were on our way to visit.

Mr. Churchill didn't seem at all put out by the prospect. He spent most of the journey talking with his Personal Private Secretary, a very smooth and elegant-looking man, whom I had rarely noticed at Chartwell. Whoever he was, his world and ours did not coincide and I don't believe he ever addressed a word to me. (From now on I will refer to him, whenever he crops up in this story as Mr. PPS.) Winston and I bounced about on our seats and passed the time playing games or making faces at each other.

What was the point of taking us to Chequers? For the experience? No - Mr. Attlee had young visitors too and there was an idea that we would all have tea and maybe play together in the garden. It was raining and it didn't turn out like that at all. Winston and I were welcomed into the house by Mr. Attlee himself, a very soft and mild mannered man who wore the same kind of parliamentary uniform that Mr. Churchill was wearing. He suggested that Winston and I would probably be quite comfortable sitting on two upright chairs in the hallway for a short while because he and Mr. Churchill had a couple of things to discuss and they wouldn't keep us waiting for more than five minutes or so. Did we bring something to read?

The hallway was large. It was long and imposing with carved wooden pillars placed here and there which contributed to the effect of grandness, but there was no sign of paintwork anywhere. Actually, I cannot remember what colour the ceiling was, but the walls in the hallway were emphatically dark brown. There were panels of polished wood everywhere which smelled waxy-clean and rather forbidding. Leading off the hallway were a couple of imposing wooden doors and there was a wide wooden staircase somewhere at the far end of the hallway. There was nothing for us to do, nothing to read, nothing to look at. No sign of Mr. Attlee's young visitors. No sign of Mr. PPS even. The dark and gloomy character of the place soon got to us and we quickly became restless. We were very, very bored. I got up once to go for a little explore, and began to venture across the massive embroidered rug which covered part of the wooden floor, to get a better sense of the geography of the ground floor. Winston stopped me as soon as I stood up. "Sit down" he commanded. " My grandfather wants to know that we can be trusted to do what we're told. Whatever do you think you're doing?"

This seemed altogether out of character from the boy who, on other occasions, liked to present himself as something of an iconoclast and boast about his rebellious nature. How many times had I been forced to listen to the various acts of deviance and defiance he claimed he had committed, very few of which I had actually witnessed? On this occasion I did what he wanted and said nothing - but I knew very well what this particular pattern of behaviour was about. It had everything to do with the importance Winston attached to his relationship with his grandfather. I had become aware that Winston's grandfather played a massively significant, yet complex, part in his life - not too entirely different, after all, from the part that my own grandfather was playing in mine. But right now I could see that Winston wanted Mr. Churchill's love and approval more than anything else in the world. It was central to him, and mattered a very great deal. I think this need was instrumental in driving the way he conducted himself at Chartwell. Maybe I sensed that all his little attention-seeking exploits and the snuffling, bad-boy image he liked to cultivate were somehow designed to win his grandfather's attention, and, in time, his admiration. But I was an eight-year-old kid, no better than him, and certainly no expert in child psychology.

When I first went to Chartwell in that summer of 1949 Winston and I had just left Gibbs, the pre-prep school in London featuring the remarkable Miss Harvey. We had both been accepted at our respective prep schools to start in September and this was going to mean living away from home, "boarding" as it was called. Winston was going to a school called Ludgrove, near Wokingham somewhere, and I was going to Elstree School, a prep school that had vacated the place called Elstree (near London) in the war and had also taken root in the Berkshire countryside, not far from Newbury. There were eighty boys at Elstree school when I was there. I was relieved to find that, in comparison with my new classmates, I was quite good at most of the school subjects, especially English and Latin, but pretty hopeless at Maths. There were plenty of team sports as well as a great expanse of rolling parkland where we could create adventures and roam around as much as we liked at appointed times on Sunday afternoons in the summer term. I loved being there and was completely taken up with a whole cluster of new friends and the raft of new challenges which the school provided. I didn't give Winston, or my visit to Chartwell, a moment's thought.

Sometime in the course of my first Easter holidays from Elstree, my mother told me that she had taken a telephone call from Mrs. Churchill's private secretary. Penelope had given her what to me sounded the most extraordinary message. Apparently, so my mother reported it, Penelope had said : "Following Jonathan's most successful visit to Chartwell last summer, Mrs. Churchill wondered whether he would like to come to stay at Chartwell again during next summer's holiday? Mrs. Churchill was hoping" Penelope had continued, "that he and Winston would come and stay towards the end of July. Would you have a word with Jonathan and let me know what you decide?"

What I found so odd about the message, so completely unexpected, were the words "Jonathan's most successful visit". In what ways, I wondered, did anybody consider my visit to have been a success? Did Winston know about this? Apart from the little pleasures he derived from playing dreary one-upmanship games with me, I found it hard to believe that he would want to spend so much time in my company again. For we really were not the best of friends - we didn't have much in common, and we wouldn't have seen each other or communicated with each other for at least twelve months. And now we were at different schools we didn't even have the shared experience of Miss Harvey's great lessons. It was all a bit of a mystery.

Perhaps Mrs. Churchill thought it would be better to have a friend of Winston staying who knew the house, knew the family, and knew the pattern of life at Chartwell, the ritual of 12.45 drinks-before-lunch and so on. I really don't know and I don't want to start guessing. Secretly - but perversely - I felt rather touched, proud almost, to think that Mr. and Mrs. Churchill might want to see me again, and after looking at all the pros and cons with my Mum, we agreed that, in spite of the fact that Winston and I would probably never become bosom friends, I would be happy to go to Chartwell again, and that she would ring Penelope and tell her as much.

4

JULY 1950
(SECOND VISIT)

That summer term at Elstree was especially good:
plenty of cricket, some new subjects, getting used to
each of my teachers' little ways, end of year exams
and then, almost before I was ready for it, the summer
holidays arrived. And for ten days in July I would be going
back to Chartwell. Was I looking forward to it? Well, I
wasn't *not* looking forward to it. It would be interesting
to see if Winston had changed at all after his year at
Ludgrove, and it would be fun to see if I was any more
competent with the grouse, or with whatever complicated
dish we might be given to cope with. I certainly wasn't
dreading it.

When Winston and I arrived at Chartwell, we were
told that this time we would not be sleeping at Orchard
Cottage, but that we would be sharing a bedroom on
the second floor of Chartwell itself. We would have our
breakfast and a light supper each day by ourselves in
another room just a few yards along the corridor on the
second floor. The bedroom was a lovely big room with big
windows and a wash basin in one corner. Two single beds

well spaced away from each other occupied the middle section of the room and I remember a large wardrobe and a chest of drawers for our clothes. It felt good to be accommodated in the house rather than down at the bottom of the garden, and although Grace Hamblin had been extraordinarily pleasant and kind to us at Orchard Cottage, I imagined that we would now feel closer to the pulse of whatever was going on.

This was July 1950 - I had reached the ripe old age of nine and a half. The general election which had taken place earlier in February was, of course, the election which Mr. Churchill had been preparing for on that day on the balcony of Hyde Park Gate when he had held my hand. As he had rightly predicted, the Conservative Party lost that election, although not by a very large margin, and Mr. Attlee was still Prime Minister. And so I wondered whether, with no general election coming up Mr. Churchill might have a little bit more leisure, more time to potter about the garden perhaps, maybe even join in a game of French cricket with Winston and me.

One morning we saw the big black sedan parked outside the front door and Winston and I knew that something was up. Could this be Mr. Churchill going to London, or flying to Paris, or going off to see Mr. Attlee again? Something like that? Please, we both hoped, if he was going to see Mr. Attlee, would he NOT take us with him.

There was another reason why we didn't want to be taken out in the car. Soon after we arrived at Chartwell on this occasion - I think it was on our second day, in fact - Penelope had come over to us while we were sitting on the grass talking about school and subjects and masters and things. She was carrying a very long, thin parcel with her, long enough to make me think of fishing rods . . . or a pair of crutches. She said: "Here you are, boys. Mrs. Churchill asked me to bring these out to you." And it turned out that Penelope had been carrying two identical parcels, one for Winston and the other one for me.

My parcel, like Winston's, contained a most beautiful set of bow and arrows, the most amazing present I had ever received . The bow was made out of some kind of metal and then painted a gorgeous light blue colour. I can see and feel it still. The metal shaft of the bow would bend and flex itself perfectly in response to pressure when you fixed the arrow and pulled the wire cord back towards your shoulder. Winston's was exactly the same. The tips of each arrow-head were blunt but you wouldn't want to get one in the eye. Come to think of it, you wouldn't want to get one anywhere much - either above your neck or below it. Penelope had said we were to be very careful not to point the arrows at each other, but I have a feeling she was half way back to the house with her back turned away from us when she said it. Never mind - we were older and wiser than we had been last year, and would no doubt do our best to be careful. At Linkenholt my grandfather was always fond of stressing the importance of gun safety - he was thinking of shotguns, of course - and insisted that Robert and I learn the many verses of the doggerel poem which begins "Never, never let your gun/Pointed be at anyone/That it may unloaded be/Matters not the least to me." I thought Winston might be impressed by this, make the connection between shotguns and bows and arrows and agree not to use his present as a lethal weapon against me or anyone else who happened to be walking by. If he was impressed by my recitation he managed not to show it.

We had the greatest fun. We invented a range of competitions: who could shoot the farthest, the highest, the straightest and so forth. Who could hit a target, a tin can, a flying sparrow a stick thrown up onto the air

. . . and on it went. We were having such a good time -
why would we want to go off in the car and have our
ambitions to become that day's *victor ludorum* thwarted?
However, after an earlier than usual lunch Mrs. Churchill
told us that any plans we might have developed for the
afternoon would have to be postponed. That was because
this afternoon we were all going in the car to Blenheim
Palace to have tea with John, Duke of Marlborough who
was Mr. Churchill's cousin, so we had better pop upstairs
have a bit of a wash and a clean-up and get ready to leave
in fifteen minutes.

Blenheim really did seem a huge distance away from
Chartwell. Winston and I were polite and well-behaved
for a large part of the long journey, and luckily just as
that dreadful combination of tiredness and car-sickness
began to set in we arrived at our destination. And what a
destination! We drove up the huge Great Court to a door
on one side of the rectangular courtyard and were shown
into a very smart drawing room, still on the ground floor
but overlooking one side of the gardens with a view of the
parkland beyond. The adults all sat down on comfortable
silk-covered armchairs, and there was at least one sofa too.
Tea was brought in upon a quite large trolley. And what a
superb tea it was: there were sandwiches of different kinds,
homemade biscuits and at least two cakes to choose from
in addition to a grand silver pot of tea and lots of milk and
lemonade for the boys. It was suggested, I think by Mrs.
Churchill, that Winston and I would be better off sitting
on two upright chairs within easy reach of a table, so that
we wouldn't make too much of a mess. I think I must have
missed Aunt Jane's training session on How to Balance a
Small Plate with Sandwiches and Cup of Tea Together in
One Hand because I wouldn't have had the first idea how
to do it. But it didn't matter at all because Winston and I

were well placed, balance was provided by the table we were sitting at, and we began tucking in to the delicious food that had been provided.

I wish I could give a vivid account of the tea party. A witty sketch of the Duke and Duchess of Marlborough, perhaps, or some well-observed insight into the warmth of the relationship between the cousins. Maybe, if all else fails, a list - just the bare bones of a list - hinting at some of the topics that were discussed as Winston and I went about the serious business of filling our faces with cake. It's most disappointing to discover that while I may have a good memory for the yummy squidge of a cucumber sandwich, when it comes to matters of a more wide-reaching nature, matters of state, for instance, the gold standard, defence cuts, national security, or house-building programmes, my mind goes completely blank. Actually, what had happened - and not for the first time - was that Mrs. Churchill had cleverly steered Winston and me away from such meaty conversation to a nice big trough where two little piggies could snort away together quite contentedly. This way no one had to bother with involving us in any of the chat. Indeed, there was no need for anyone to address a single word to us. Except Mrs. Churchill, of course. And so when we had quite finished our tea, Mrs. Churchill came over to our table and suggested that it might be a good idea if we were to go into the garden and look around for a short time before the long drive back to Chartwell. The French doors leading out into the garden were opened for us and, wishing I hadn't succumbed to that second slice of coffee cake, I followed Winston out onto the lawn.

Maybe it was the cake, or maybe it was the strangeness and the hugeness of Blenheim, or maybe it was withdrawal symptoms from my bow and arrows - I don't know what it was, but the next quarter of an hour wasn't much fun.

No sooner had Winston and I begun to mooch around the lawns and borders than we slipped back into the bad, old, destructive patterns of the previous summer. Immediately I felt oddly disconnected from myself as the person I had become used to being with my friends at Elstree. When Winston challenged me, in that familiar jokey style of his which had plenty of edge to it, to assess how my grandfather and Linkenholt would compare with his grandfather and Blenheim and so on, I suddenly felt I was in the wrong place altogether. I was nine and a half and pretty certain to be captain of the Under Eleven cricket team next year - why was I wasting time listening to this rubbish? I was conscious that Mr. and Mrs. Churchill might be watching us out of the drawing room window and this was clearly not the place for Winston and me to start a big fight. So we ambled along together, an amiable and companionable sight (I hoped) from a distance, but I felt out of sorts and unnatural, uncomfortable in my skin. It was one of the first times, and I hoped it would be one of the last, when I became vividly aware of myself as playing a part, a part that I really didn't like. I felt phoney, inauthentic. Here I was, acting a character whom I knew all right, but one with whom, on this particular late summer's afternoon, I had nothing in common. But I just made myself get on with it and give this performance to the best of my ability without saying anything about it to Winston. Because this was the character I sensed that Mr. and Mrs. Churchill expected to see. Acting parts? Not much fun really.

Mrs. Churchill was consistently warm and kind to me. Not warm in any physical cuddly sense - that was not her style at all. Rather she demonstrated warmth through an outpouring of real pleasure when her attention was focused upon you. She made you feel that it was both

special and a delight for her to be in your company and
to be talking with you. So very many of my feelings of
happiness and content at Chartwell were due to the soft
glitter of brilliance which shone in her eyes and animated
her personality when she was with you. This was more
than mere charm - there was a diamond-like solidity
behind any mere manners.

Mrs. Churchill

Throughout the many hours I spent in her company
in the dining room at Chartwell I came to recognise some
of the ways Mrs. Churchill's family relied on her, not
just for her familial love and affection and not just for
her extraordinary skills - it seemed to me - as household
manager. But all the members of her family that I met
seemed to value, if not depend upon, the rock-solid

strength of her character. Mrs. Churchill did not attempt to mask the strength of her convictions, nor the importance she attached to the values which informed her daily life. Sometimes Mr. Churchill would appear to be uncertain whether a point he had just made in conversation was altogether acceptable or whether it betrayed a flawed or dubious moral outlook. On some of these occasions he would look across at Mrs. Churchill sitting at the other end of the long table, with a beseeching almost plaintive look that, when I think of it, still touches me. The look said first how much he loved her, and second how much he needed her thoughts and guidance on the matter in question that he didn't feel altogether certain about.

Mrs. Churchill had a little word with Winston and me at the beginning of my second stay at Chartwell. I am probably deceiving myself, but she seemed to be as warmly disposed to me as she did to Winston, but then she was inclined - when I was with him - to treat Winston and me as if we were two people but one unit, joined at the hip. Mrs. Churchill explained that Mr. Churchill would not be fighting an election this year, but that, nevertheless, he would be busy writing his "History of the English Speaking Peoples" and we still should try to stay out of his way in the mornings. "You'll see him", she said, "at luncheon whenever he's here. Probably best", she went on, "to continue to think of his rooms as being out of bounds for the rest of the summer at least". It was funny, I thought, that although she had never told me it was "out of bounds" I had never been into Mrs. Churchill's side of the house and I had no idea how many rooms there might be in what amounted to her private apartments there. In just the same way I had never been into Mr. Churchill's "rooms" and imagined I never would - so his big study and his writing desk, his secretary and her typewriter and bookcases stacked with books and papers would all have to remain figments of my imagination.

Another room in the house which I never visited during my first visit to Chartwell was the Cinema. I think it was Mary Soames who had asked us last year whether we had been shown any films yet, and of course we hadn't. But I was left wondering where on earth in the house the Cinema Room was located and what kind of an experience this would be.

There were other places, too, where Winston and I never ventured. I would have very much liked to have visit the kitchens, but Winston was against it. When Robert and I went for our holidays to Linkenholt we stayed - obviously - in the big house with Granny and Grandpop. Granny had developed a routine each morning whereby after breakfast she would walk down one of the passages on the ground floor of the house to a big walk-in larder equipped with table and chairs, for her daily meeting with Mrs. Hawkins, the cook. There were glass-fronted cupboards all round the room, and Granny and Mrs. Hawkins would plan their menus while Rob and I, who often came too, would listen and gaze in wonder at the enormous jars of bottled fruit which were stored on shelves behind the closed cupboard doors. This was fun, not only because Mrs. Hawkins spoilt us and made sure we got tit-bits of her chocolate or toffee to taste, but because Granny would inevitably finish the meeting by walking back with Mrs. Hawkins into the kitchen itself. Here we could glimpse great haunches of ham tied up to giant hooks in the ceiling; in the shooting season pairs of partridges and brace of pheasants would be hanging undercover outside the pantry; Tom might come in with the vegetables he had been asked to bring to the house that morning - and get a cup of tea and a chat for his pains; and there was a very big kitchen range along one side of the room over which was suspended a contraption of ropes and pulleys. This was a clothes dryer, and there was usually a colourful collection of Granny and Grandpop's clothes hanging up to dry.

There were other delights associated with a visit to the kitchen at Linkenholt: above all, it was a warm and cosy place, a place where people without pretension did good work with kitchen knives, metal ladles, wooden spoons and rollers; here they made delicious-tasting roasts and stews, gravies, and puddings, cakes and biscuits. It was a sweat-of-the brow work-place, a warm-hearted place and I always loved being there. Sometimes we were invited by Mrs. Hawkins or by Mr. Head, the butler, to come through, past the kitchen, under the haunches of ham, to the staff sitting room. There we were treated politely (still plenty of Master Jonathan, Master Robert) and we sat and gossiped and brought them edited bits of news about what we boys were up to . . . . I found it refreshing to be with them although their world was strangely different from the one Rob and I were being trained in. Yet, for all that it may have been a bit strange and different, their "world" was only a few paces away from us, through a door and down a passage in the same house.

Maybe I wanted to visit the kitchen at Chartwell to experience the same kind of warm and friendly camaraderie there. It might have been a good place for us boys to go for a bit of respite from the need to be continually on our best behaviour. On the other hand, I cannot imagine Mr. or Mrs. Churchill encouraging it. Something about confidentiality . . . the Official Secrets Act . . . . MI5, MI6, Special Branch . . . Eddie's pistol under his pillow. Oh no - it would never do. But I still think, if we had been allowed or encouraged to go there, I would have liked that.

There was going to be a film show, Mrs. Churchill said, this very evening. At the appointed time we were taken down into the basement of the house, down past the kitchens, along a winding passage and there ahead of us was an open door off to our right. We went in and found ourselves at the back of quite a small rectangular room. A big screen had been erected at the front of the room and a film projector was standing towards the back, between some of the seats. As we went in I saw that the whole seating area had been created on three or four different levels, rising from the screen end towards the projector in a gentle rake. There was a platform on each level, each one carpeted like the rest of the room, and comfortable chairs had been placed in an orderly row on each one, with little tables for drinks and refreshments within reach.

Mr. and Mrs. Churchill came in after we had arrived and sat down in two seats which were specially reserved for them, Winston told me, every time there was a film show. Winston and I sat in the row in front of them, off to the side a bit, and Mary Soames and Nicholas, her husband, sat next to Mr. and Mrs. Churchill. Other people had come to watch the film too, but I didn't know who any of them were except Eddie and Penelope. I supposed the young women could have been Mr. Churchill's assistants or secretaries or maybe Mrs. Churchill's helpers. I didn't know, and I don't remember any other men being there. But I do remember the film.

This was the 1940 black and white adaptation of "Pride and Prejudice" with Greer Garson playing Elizabeth Bennet and Laurence Olivier playing Mr. Darcy. I had never read a Jane Austen novel and I had never seen a film quite like this. It was extraordinary and held my attention despite the number of reasons why I should be thoroughly fed up with it. There were too many rather hopeless young women, for a start, all - except Elizabeth - rather too simpering and dependent on menfolk for my taste. "Wet" was the word I would have used to describe them. The men weren't very much more agreeable, I thought. Nanny would have disliked Darcy I was sure: "thinks himself so superior" would probably have been her verdict, while Mr. Bingley seemed a good bit too pleased with himself, and too little interested in anything much else, to form a decent attachment to Jane. Oh dear, the story was getting so complicated. I thought Mr. Darcy looked wonderfully handsome in his frilly shirts, especially when he was standing, as he often seemed to be, against bowers and arches and trellises all decked out with climbing roses in full bloom. And although you couldn't tell what colour the roses were, you could, if you happened to be Mr. and Mrs. Churchill, tell a lot about the variety. It was quite easy to tell the colour of a particular rose, Mrs. Churchill said, if you happened to know, as she did, something about the variety.

Mr. and Mrs. Churchill were having such a good time together. No one there with us in the cinema that evening could have been in any doubt about that: for while it may have been the convention in commercial cinemas to be reasonably quiet, and keep your chat level - if you had to talk at all while the film was running - to a whisper, here at Chartwell, in their own private cinema, Mr. and Mrs. Churchill clearly felt they could talk as much and as loudly as they wanted. And they did.

No amount of knowledge about rose varieties would have helped them know what on earth was going on behind Mr. Darcy's puckered brows, as Laurence Olivier stood there, braced against the high pollen count, lace handkerchief at the ready, looking bemused and out of sorts as the light wind ruffled his frilly shirt. Mr. and Mrs.

Churchill, with Mary and Nicholas Soames joining in the
fun as well, loved watching this film. They knew Jane
Austen's story well, so the narrative in this adaptation
did not take them too much by surprise but when it did
- and apparently Aldous Huxley and his co-writer had
messed about with the story a fair bit - Mr. Churchill let
us know in no uncertain terms what he thought of the
changes. Nor was Mr. Churchill always happy with the
richness of the style - it was he who usually led the critical
commentary and he was very, very funny when he was
finding fault with something. The whole room would
begin laughing, and then it got more and more difficult
for everyone to stop.

Laughter was not at all in evidence the next time
we went to a film show. This time it was a film about
war, a relentless (I thought) series of impressions of
horror and distress. It too was in black and white and
I remember shootings, barricades and bombardments
with masses of people losing their homes or getting
wounded or just dying. It was grim stuff, and I did not
dare turn my head and see how Mr. and Mrs. Churchill
were taking it. Mr. Churchill had said nothing at all
until suddenly, in the middle of one scene, that changed.
It was a scene of flight: a great many men and women
running together away from something terrible that was
going on behind them, and as they ran, too many for
the narrow street they were in, one of the men - maybe
a leading character in the film, but I think not - tripped
and fell. As he crashed to the ground his rather frail-
looking wire spectacles fell from his face and, in the
chaos of everyone running and jostling, were accidently
crushed by the boot of one of his compatriots. It was a
shocking moment, the director managed to frame the
boot coming down on the spectacles in a way which held

the moment and maximised the dramatic impact. For Mr. Churchill this moment seemed to underline more than a dramatic *coup de theatre*. His exclamation of sympathy for the fallen man, now without any means of sight, was accompanied by a sigh which seemed to suggest an overwhelming despair at the suffering and loss of everyone who was ever devastated by war. The few words which Mr. Churchill uttered were, I am sure, intended to reach beyond this particular character in this black and white artefact of a film and extend compassion not just to the one or to the few, but to the hundreds and to the thousands. It is true - I could easily be inventing this interpretation from the few simple words which Mr. Churchill exclaimed, but I was arrested by the harrowing effect of his tone and delivery. Soon after Mr. Churchill's intervention I heard him strike a match and the familiar smell of his cigar smoke began to waft across to where we were sitting.

Now - what on earth was the film? I am putting my money on All Quiet on the Western Front (1930), Lewis Milestone's award winning epic. But, I cannot confirm whether that scene featuring the trampling of the spectacles appears in it or not.

I don't think I ever saw Mr. Churchill smoke an entire cigar. More usually, in my presence at least, he would light a new cigar with a tremendous display of huffing and puffing and rolling the cigar round his fingers as he sucked, then take a couple of puffs, then leave it to go out. Very often he would come into the room carrying an unlit cigar in his hand, one that he had lit previously, and one that he intended to light again at some time in the near future. I suspect that he did most of his smoking in the privacy of his own quarters, maybe while reading in bed, or while dictating his book. Certainly the atmosphere in the hallway, the staircase and the dining room did not seem heavy with cigar smoke, although I have the impression that Mr. Churchill did allow himself a puff or two in all of these places.

There was to be a special evening before my time at Chartwell was up and I had to go home: Winston and I were going to stay up for dinner with Mr. and Mrs. Churchill in the dining room. Mary Soames would be coming, but no-one else was invited. It was to be a farewell dinner, and a chance for me in particular, and Winston too, I supposed, to say thank-you to Mrs. Churchill for making our holiday such fun - and especially for the bows and arrows with which we had dominated the garden and terrified the life out of anyone who hadn't expected to walk into a re-run of the Battle of Agincourt. We were to wear our long trousers and jackets, and scrub up for the occasion.

The dinner was really lovely. The table was candle-lit with the silver peacocks and pheasants glinting as if they were preening in honour of this feast. We had clear consommé soup to begin followed by roast chicken and mashed potatoes - an absolute favourite - and summer pudding and cream to finish off. It was special, and it seemed as if everyone had something that they really enjoyed. I was put to sit next to Mr. Churchill on his left and Winston sat on his right. Throughout the meal Mr. Churchill beamed away at both of us, not asking me too many questions - for obvious reasons - but telling us about real turtle soup and Napoleon Bonaparte and how Boney should have found a better way to relax than to declare war upon the British Army.

Mr. Churchill

There was a benign twinkle in Mr. Churchill's eyes as he looked at us. He would talk calmly and pleasantly to me and when he did ask me to tell him things, these were usually things about my father or my grandfather. He said he would be interested to hear what regiment my father had served in, where exactly he was killed, what do I remember about him and so on and so forth. He was really lovely to me and, not unlike my grandfather, comically gruff and boisterous when he sensed that my own part of the conversation was getting a bit bogged down. He wanted to know about Linkenholt, too - it was as if the dreaded fishmonger episode had been forgotten, thank goodness - and I could happily tell him about the farm and the tractors and all the new machinery that Grandpop had either brought in from Switzerland or else invented himself. I told him how much I had enjoyed

the figs off his own fig tree on the south facing wall at
Chartwell and how we didn't have figs at Linkenholt.
When I told him about my grandfather's obsessive drive
to get his greengage tree to produce fruit he smiled happily
- maybe, I thought, at the recognition of another obstinate
old buffer showing the world some spirit.

After dinner, Mr. Churchill drank some brandy, had
a puff or two of his cigar and sat back as if to digest
and ponder the childish world that Winston and I still
inhabited. He did not sit back for long. His peace was
interrupted, he himself might have said shattered, by a very
loud intervention from the other end of the table. Mary
Soames, always so enthusiastic and encouraging to both
Winston and me, had, I think, noticed her father enjoying
his conversations during dinner. He had not, as I suspect
she had feared he might, become bored or distracted. And
so, without actually standing up, pinging a wine glass with
her fork, or clapping her hands she stopped everything
and everyone with a loud cry of "Daddy!" When Mr.
Churchill looked up, she went on "Daddy, wouldn't this
be a good moment? Mummy and I think this would be an
excellent moment, and I know we would all be delighted
if you would tell the boys one of your Boer War stories!
Why don't you?"

And that was it. Mr. Churchill quickly realised that
the situation now required him to fight off post-prandial
reflection and contemplation and, like the old actor that
he was, get himself gee'd up for another performance of
his once-seen-never-forgotten "Boer War". He finished off
all but a drop of his brandy, took the little-smoked cigar
out of his mouth and put it, soggy side down, into the
brandy glass. Next he reached out to collect a glittering
array of fellow actors who, although cast in strictly non-
speaking parts, were given important roles requiring them

to provide fiendish cunning and surprise attack as well as
dead and wounded bodies. The silverware on my side of
the table comprised Salt, White Pepper, Mustard, Black
Pepper mill, Pheasant and Toothpicks, and Mr. Churchill
had a similar troupe of silverware available on the other
side of the table, where Winston was sitting, if he should
need to call upon them.

The story Mr. Churchill told us, with thrilling flourishes
of dramatic narration, was about an episode from his own
early life. Mr. Churchill was in his twenties and working
in South Africa as a war reporter for one of the great
London newspapers in such a way that he could combine
his desire for adventure with a laudable ambition for
fame and fortune. This was the time when the Boers were
being put under pressure to surrender their lands and gold
deposits to the British - but of course the Boers wouldn't
agree to that, and they developed a campaign of guerrilla
warfare to outwit the British Army. So at the time his story
began Mr. Churchill was loosely attached to a British
regiment whose spies had led the regiment to confront a
sizeable section of Boer forces. Equipped with a pistol at
his belt and a sabre holstered at his back ready for use
at any moment, Mr. Churchill took up a position on a
promontory above the Boer camp where he would have
a perfect view of the skirmish that was bound to ensue.

While I might have benefitted had Miss Harvey spent
half an hour explaining the ins and outs of the Boer War
to me before this holiday at Chartwell, my poor command
of the basic history of the period didn't, I believe, matter
too much on this particular evening. Because knowing the
history really wasn't the point. The point, I believed, would
become clear so long as I could keep up with the vivid uses
that Mr. Churchill made of the non-speaking parts. It was
mesmerising. No sooner had White Pepper (Mr. Churchill)

taken up his position on high ground, there came a fearful volley of gunfire from the Pheasant and Toothpicks (Boers) directed at the Salt and Mustard (British Line). The Salt and Mustard found themselves hopelessly exposed and there were casualties. (More pieces of silverware were brought across the table to work as "casualties"). White Pepper felt duty-bound "to leave my position, and set off at a gallop towards the wooded headland" where the Salt and Mustard were holding on. When the Black Pepper mill (Boers reserve) was brought into the action, White Pepper immediately saw what was going to happen "and there was nothing for it but to draw my sabre and set my horse to gallop full tilt at the leader of the enemy reserve . . . ."

Mr. Churchill delivered the exciting story with all the rhetorical tricks of a 19th Century actor-manager, and moving the pieces of silverware gave him added scope to enliven the physical aspects. The story got more intricate but it continued in this vein for some time until it became clear that the Boer assaults, front and rear, were going to produce a resounding victory - Mr. Churchill only managed to escape capture by scrambling through dense undergrowth in a nearby wood. But the pieces of highly polished silver tableware had suffered too: some were knocked over onto the table, dead or mortally wounded; some looked drained, their complexions dulled by the bruising speed of foot they had been forced to employ in Mr. Churchill's hands. Only the Pheasant retained something of a sparkle in its plumage. But then the Pheasant (with the support of the Toothpicks and the Black Pepper mill) had won the day.

After breakfast on the last morning, Mrs. Churchill took me up to Mr. Churchill's rooms. She knocked lightly on the door of what turned out to be his bedroom, and there was Mr. Churchill sitting up in bed with spectacles on nose and different sets of typed papers and documents lying all around him on the bedclothes. There were two other people in the room with him, I noticed: a young woman with a short-hand notepad and the distinguished-looking Mr. PPS whose real name I didn't know. Mr. Churchill turned his head towards the door in what was clearly an awkward position for his neck and looked over his specs towards Mrs. Churchill who said "Jonathan has come to say goodbye to you. His mother and step-father are coming to collect him just before luncheon." And she left me there, standing in the doorway.

Mr. Churchill called me into the room and told me to shut the door. He asked whether I had enjoyed being at Chartwell, and this was enough to enable me to launch myself into the short speech I had prepared earlier for just such an occasion as this. So I went ahead with "Yes it's been tremendous fun and thank you very much for inviting me" and a bit more but not too much more. Luckily I didn't get stuck on any of the words, and I could reflect afterwards that perhaps this was because I had had such a happy and funny time when he told us about his adventures in the Boer War.

Mr. Churchill then said "Look, Jonathan, I have written in this book for you and I would like you to take it away and maybe you will read it one day". And he began to fish about among the paperwork on his bed and Mr. PPS came over to help and they soon found the copy of "My Early Life" which Mr. Churchill had inscribed in preparation for my visit. I thanked him and he said a grandfatherly goodbye, tender and kind, with a big hint of Let-us-not-drag-this-out-too-long in what I thought might be called his crumpled face.

I found my way back to the familiar territory of our bedroom, and put the book in my small suitcase with the

rest of the things that I had packed. Richard, my step-
father, and Mummy would be arriving at around noon I
was told, so Winston and I had a bit of time for at least
one more archery competition - maybe a best of 5, or
maybe even a best of 21 if my parents were late in getting
here. We had just set up the tin bucket in our favourite
place, and were measuring out our agreed distance when
Penelope appeared. She didn't want to interrupt, she said,
but she'd like to say goodbye since this was my last day
for what she called "another year". She wanted to say
how I'd been the perfect guest, etcetera, etcetera and she
hoped I'd had a good time. "I'm glad", she said, "that the
bows and arrows have been a success. Jonathan, if you
have no further use for yours, why don't you leave it with
Winston's when you go home?"

Now I cannot swear that those were her actual words,
but Penelope clearly intended that I should leave my bow
and arrows here at Chartwell. From my point of view
this was extremely disappointing: I had begun to regard
them as my own personal property, and was planning to
take them home, show them to Rob, maybe take them
to Linkenholt and play with them there. Were they not
a gift from Mrs. Churchill to me personally to do with
whatsoever I wanted? I couldn't bear the idea of leaving
the precious things behind. But wait a minute - had
not Penelope just said to me "if you have no further use
for yours"? Well, I did have further use for mine as it
happened, and if anybody objected to my plan to take
them away with me I would simply tell a lie: I would say
I must have misunderstood what Penelope was telling me.
Fool that I was, I decided to test the idea out by telling
Winston what I planned to do.

Winston would have none of it. It was monstrous,
he said, that I should even consider taking the bow and

arrows away from Chartwell. His Granny had bought
the bows and arrows for us to play with, sure, but they
were her property, not his and certainly not mine, a mere
visitor. They belonged here at Chartwell and when I was
long gone and forgotten, other children who might come
to Chartwell would find them here among the other games
that Granny had bought over the years and would enjoy
playing with them. Winston was angry, very angry, but he
spoke with absolute clarity and made his point well. It
was a devilishly good point too, I could see that. He even
suggested that, if I did take the bow and arrows away with
me that very day, I would be regarded as a thief, stealing
property that did not belong to me.

I felt dismayed that Winston saw it like this. We had
argued and fought over a great many issues during the
times we had spent together at Chartwell, and now here
was another one, but another one with a difference. It was
different because on this one, my conscience screamed,
Winston was in the right and I was definitely in the wrong.
But over the weeks that we had shared a bedroom and
shared time together, we had, even though we didn't really
get on, developed a satisfactory way of coping with our
rows and disagreements. "Never Yield" and "Never Admit
You're Wrong" were two of our guiding principles, and
they had served us well. Whenever we argued, we ended
the argument by agreeing to differ. This did nothing to
bring us closer together, but it did ensure that nobody won
and nobody lost face. There was no giving-in. And no
gloating. But I was having to live with the fact that, where
conscience was involved, there might be consequences I
hadn't yet considered.

Richard's black saloon car turned into the drive at
noon, and, as expected, out stepped Richard and Mummy.
But there was a third person still sitting in the back seat,

and to my great delight, I realised it was Nanny! This
was so wonderful - Nanny here at Chartwell! But what a
resounding pity: I had already said my goodbyes to Mr.
Churchill, and Nanny would therefore miss out on seeing
her hero, the "Great Man" as she had once described him
to me. Mrs. Churchill had arranged for the drinks trolley to
be present in its usual place from noon onwards, and now
she invited Mummy, Richard and Nanny to come up the
stairs to the landing where she proceeded to offer everyone
refreshments. Mummy was talking to Mrs. Churchill with
Richard at her side, so Winston and I were able to sit with
Nanny. I offered her a taste of my delicious tomato juice
(she had chosen Barley Water), and I jabbered excitedly in
my joy at seeing her. Suddenly I noticed that Richard was
standing up and for a fleeting second I wondered if he was
making a move to go. But it wasn't that. Coming round the
corner, quite slowly and deliberately as was his way, was
Mr. Churchill himself. He stopped and made a little speech
of greeting to the newcomers, maybe something like, "I
have come to welcome you here to Chartwell, something
I know Clemmie will have done already, but welcome is
one of life's little courtesies that cannot be overdone. I
am indeed very happy to welcome you all here today"
- and he waited for Mrs. Churchill to make the verbal
introductions which she did with her characteristic poise
and charm. Mr. Churchill shook hands with my mother
and then with Richard, and then - I found my heart was
in my mouth - with Nanny!

I left Nanny talking with Mr. Churchill and with
Winston while I went out with Richard down the stairs
into the entrance hall where I had left my suitcase ready
for loading into the car. Richard opened the boot and
took the suitcase from me. I said "Could you just hold on
a minute?" and popped back into the hall where we had

left the bows and arrows. "What's this?" Richard said and I told him Mrs. Churchill had given it to me as a present and that I was going to take it to Linkenholt. He laid my bow and the arrows across the floor of the boot, and shut the lid with a bang just as Mr. and Mrs. Churchill came out of the front door with Mummy, Nanny and Winston. I had already said my proper goodbye and thank-you to Mr. and Mrs. Churchill, together and separately. It remained only to say goodbye to Winston.

I felt really, really bad about it. Sick with shame. But there was no going back.

5

AFTERWARDS

Robert and I had a good time at Linkenholt when we got there. We never played with the bow and arrows. Aunt Jane may have been looking after us at the time and if so I expect she forbade us to play with them unattended on the grounds that they were too dangerous. I didn't want to play with them anyway. Robert couldn't understand why I hadn't left the stupid things at Chartwell. I didn't want to see them again.

One afternoon I found Grandpop reading my end of year school report. He was thoroughly entitled to do this because it was he, not my mother, who was paying the school fees and anyway it was he who expressed the most interest about my development at school and my aptitude at academic subjects. I had finished my first year at Elstree in early July - it was now September 1st - and we sat down together and he congratulated me on the year's report. He picked out my best subjects, remarked pointedly that mathematics was not one of these, and said "so, my boy - what do you intend to do with yourself when you grow up and leave school or university?"

O Lord! It didn't seem possible! Two questions about my future from distinguished grand-father figures, neither of which I felt in a position to answer satisfactorily. I had made a great hash of the first answer a year ago - best to play it more cautiously with Grandpop, be a little more vague and uncertain. Because the truth was that it felt much too early to identify a career, or even a way of life. There were too many things troubling me: for a start, what would I be any good at in the grown-up world of work? Would I be able to cope with it, with the dreaded stammer and everything? I may have done comparatively well in my first year at prep school, and for sure I was very happy there, but prep school seemed miles away from having to make choices about adult careers and stuff like that. Maybe I'd just have to wait, like Theseus in Miss Harvey's captivating story, until I felt strong and manly enough to move that heavy boulder and see what was underneath.

I was looking serious all right but not offering Grandpop anything in the way of a reply. He tried again to get me to focus my thoughts on his question: "Jonny - were you listening to me?" I nodded.   "All right - take your time. We're not in a hurry." Don't be rude, I told myself, say something which will please your grandfather, but make it a bit vague and wobbly. Say something bland, but keep your mouth shut and your powder dry about the things that you're worried about. Then I wondered if this shouldn't rather be keep your mouth dry and your powder shut. Because my mouth had a worrying tendency to go dry whenever this wretched subject was raised.

There was something else worrying me too. I wasn't at all sure I would be comfortable owning a big house with huge gardens and a swimming pool, or running a big farm with massive combine harvesters and eating strawberries and grapes from my own heated greenhouses. I was pretty sure I didn't want to have people working for me if that meant ascribing some kind of inferior status to them by calling them "Hawkins" or "Burden".

I sensed at this time that there was a brittle quality in my social relationships with grown-ups. I think that's why I liked school term time so much more than holidays. Holidays had somehow become associated with the exercise of polite behaviour. It felt sometimes as if I was giving one performance after another, each one judged for its correctness by Aunt Jane and other adults who thought the way she did. It seemed to matter a great deal to these people that such arbitrary standards of class etiquette should remain intact. I didn't talk about this at all, even, I think, to Rob.

I would be back at school in a matter of days, and I was looking forward to that very much. I hoped to be playing for the Elstree Under Elevens team at football, and the match against Ludgrove next term was going to be at Ludgrove.

I knew Winston wouldn't be playing - he didn't like football, I knew that - but I wondered if he'd come and watch, maybe come and have tea with us after the game.

Silly of me, really.

EPILOGUE
WITH ACKNOWLEDGEMENTS

As a little boy I didn't keep a diary or make notes of any kind during the two successive summer holidays that I spent at Chartwell. Recently, maybe soon after I turned seventy-five, I decided to pay a visit to Chartwell in the hope that it would stimulate my memory and that the words and rhythms of actual conversations would come flooding back to me as well as particular episodes of fun, triumph, boredom or disaster that I had seen or participated in as an eight or nine-year-old. It was good to see the house again and to spend time in the garden but I'm afraid no new memories were nudged into consciousness by my being there. What memories I do have are those I have carried about with me for more than sixty-five years, and whether they have become warped with time or inflated by self-regard, whether their essence has evaporated or their integrity become compromised I really do not know. I started off thinking it would be a good idea to share what I do remember of those times with members of my family and a close band of good friends. But if these memories should happen to catch the interest and imagination of a wider readership I would, of course, be delighted.

In the process of preparing the manuscript I received considerable amounts of help and support. I owe special thanks to Sue Sabbagh, who read every draft and was kind and patient enough to suggest clever ways of improving the text at every stage of its development. When, at the outset, I was beginning to formulate a plan for writing my story, Clare Short gave me some invaluable advice about its thematic shape. Patrick Hughes read an early draft and took an enormous amount of trouble suggesting alterations to my style and presentation. My brother Robert helped by sending me a couple of good photographs from his family album, a kindness which prompted me to search more thoroughly for the photographs of Nanny and of our family which I was sure I had stored away in a safe place somewhere. (I found them eventually at the back of a bottom drawer in the spare bedroom.) I commend all these good friends whose generosity and good advice has, I believe, helped the story along in the most positive fashion.

Photographs of the Churchill family are taken from Clementine Churchill's private collection of photographs. This can be viewed at the Churchill Archives Centre, Churchill College, Cambridge. The Centre reserves all rights to these photographs, and I am grateful to the Centre for providing me with permission to use them here. Katharine Thomson and Gillian Booker, both archivists I met at the Centre, were good enough to share their knowledge and experience with me generously.

While I was at the Churchill Archives Centre I spent time attempting to verify the accuracy of names, dates, the configuration of rooms and settings as they appear in my text. I was successful in some respects, but not in all. If anyone reading this knows I have made a mistake in reporting the name of an individual, or the dates on which an episode occurs, or anything else - and is offended by it, I offer my sincere apologies. I had no desire to offend, merely to get particulars of fact as accurate as I possibly could.

*   *   *

I am greatly indebted to my mentor and editor Karl Sabbagh for believing so strongly that the story was worth writing in the first place. His editorial experience and his willingness to induct me into the world of printing and publishing have combined to give me a surprisingly painless transition from doing very little to thinking quite deeply about my childhood and then starting to write about it.

But no writing at all would have taken place were it not for the outpouring of encouragement and loving support I have received from my wife Paula. She continues to be my rock and my inspiration, and I definitely need help in finding adequate words to thank her. I have no doubt Sir Winston would have been happy to help me with this: maybe he would have given me several beautifully crafted sentences designed to encapsulate the breadth and depth of my appreciation for her. You can see, I'm sure, that without his help I am left feeling the tiniest bit tongue-tied. Well, not for the first time, eh?